May I Cut In?

A SURGEON'S STORY

Fred, at ninety years old, with the portrait his grandfather painted of him as a young man

May I Cut In?

A SURGEON'S STORY

FREDERIC PRATT HERTER, M.D.

with Ron Holland

Fred, seeking entrance

Fred, at 23 months

TABLE OF CONTENTS

Chris watching over infant Fred

Chris and Fred, the best of friends

Fred, age three, clothing free

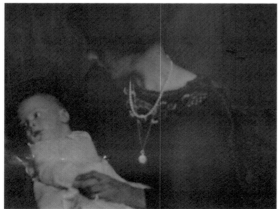

Mother and Freddie

When I took the first tentative steps toward writing this family tale, the task appeared no less than daunting. But the journey since, from the beginning right up to the present, has been a joy. Recalling one's past is interesting in itself but there's a totally unexpected bonus: one remembrance leads ineluctably to a second, but then *that* memory begets another, and soon enough, door after door opens up, and a lifetime of daily adventures stream past the mind's eye, and you're blessed with a cornucopia of forgotten details. Enough to fill days of filtering and sorting, deciding which are important or *exciting* or deserving of inclusion.

So when my brother Chris came to me with thoughts about writing something about our famous father (Dad died in 1966, much, much before his time), I jumped at the chance to help him. As did my sister Del, and our younger brother, Miles. All three of us went to work, adding our own remembrances of Dad to those of Chris. While Chris focussed primarily on our family antecedents, my slim 14 pages dealt largely with family life in the Herter home, and the part that Dad played in those idyllic days. Miles, being so much younger, had little to add, but Del wrote a sparkling replay of her constant battles with Dad, over their disparate political beliefs. (How he enjoyed that noisy jousting with his high-spirited daughter!) Somehow, Chris melded all three of our offerings into a remarkably happy and meaningful text.

That tale of Herter/Pratt doings never gained much of an audience, so Chris, encumbered by work and dogged by illness, left the task of livening it to me. But I, of course, had myriad and pressing duties in New York. To further complicate matters, part of the family history was waylaid (perhaps unconsciously by me) and what remained of the manuscript fell to the hands of Chris's grandsons, Zac and Jess Leber. They did their level best to piece the narrative together, polish the syntax and punctuation and had it bound for distribution to family members. For this they deserve and are hereby given credit. Every family member who read this scanty history was fascinated, but felt that it cried out for elaboration.

The small volume, however flawed, was of signal importance to me. It provided a priceless introduction for me to meet all manner of Herters and Pratts, and learn more of my father's brilliant public career. It was an undiluted surprise to discover how that easy-going, and even self-effacing man around our house, was a towering figure of great importance and influence around the world. Indeed, that realization became the matrix that formed much of the memoir before you.

In 1955, with my formal training and residencies behind me, I was appointed Assistant Professor of Surgery at Columbia. Three years later, having been invited to head the Department of Surgery at the American University of Beirut, Columbia promptly promoted me to Associate Professor.

Although my trip to Beirut was cancelled (thanks to the peace-making intervention of U.S. Marines in Lebanon), I nevertheless retained my promotion in rank at Columbia, for which my ever-loyal Solange gets a lot of credit. In 1965, I was made a Full Professor of Surgery. To top this off, the next year I became the first recipient of the Auchincloss Chair of Surgery. This appointment was especially meaningful to me, because I was both friend and cohort of Hugh Auchincloss, Senior, and his son, Hugh. And I wouldn't be a bit surprised if they played a role in my becoming Interim Chairman of the Surgery Department at Columbia.

These significant promotions at Columbia might suggest a full plate in my academic schedule. Not a chance. My fascination with the Middle East never faltered or wavered. In 1959, a year after my aborted invitation to spend a year on the surgical staff at AUB, I got to spend three weeks there, under the auspices of Calvin Plimpton, Chairman of the Department of Medicine. My work then was purely medical, but in my spare time, I got to know plenty about Lebanon, and its prime institute of learning. Through Dr. Plimpton, who became Chairman of the AUB Board, I managed to expand my knowledge of this American outreach, while simultaneously teaching and practicing surgery at Presbyterian Hospital in New York City.

My second career (AUB) beckoned me urgently when the Lebanese Civil War broke out in 1975. My career there was a whirlwind: In a bewildering succession, I became:

In 1977, an AUB Trustee.

In 1985, Chairman of the AUB Board.

In 1987, I was named President of the American University of Beirut.

It was a period of momentous change. The Civil War raged on until

1991, and much of my time was spent keeping the doors of AUB open, and the faculty in place. At the same time, in New York, I made certain that my patients were well and happy. So you can see there was little free time to work on Chris's family tale.

Then one fine day, out of the blue, with my Middle East and surgical careers behind me, my interest in that early family history was revived. I got a phone call from Peter Krulevitich, a distant acquaintance. He wanted me to contribute a chapter to a book he was putting together about New York City.

"Why me?", I asked, "and why New York?"

Peter answered, "Because you were born in Brooklyn."

Apparently that fact branded me a true native of Manhattan. And my age gave me close to a century's knowledge of the town where I lived and worked.

Peter guessed that I was at least 90, the cut-off age for inclusion in the book.

But Peter's guess was way off. I was a mere lad of 88, so I immediately begged off.

"No way! This is my book!" my almost-friend insisted, "And little details like your age are for me to decide. And not only that, I happen to know you wrote a book about the history of surgery at Columbia-Presbyterian Hospital and that proves you have background aplenty. And your writing is pretty damn good!"

So I gave in, though not quite happily, and did my best, offering up, on tape, my inner thoughts on New York City. Yes, I did it all orally, because Peter was adamant about that, A Dictaphone was right there to record my answers to his questions, then a typist converted my every uncertain word into a written text. Well, the mechanical part went well, but the typed-out document was anything but a success. As I read it over, in the cold light of day, I was appalled by its lack of color or humor or human interest of any sort. I called my ostensible editor, bemoaned my dissatisfaction, and asked if I might replace some of the indifferent text with more personal memories and stories.

"Go ahead," *he* said indifferently. Almost as if he'd forgotten all about the idea. So, for two long years, I worked and remembered and wrote to transform that lackluster New York history into this memoir of my own family, interlaced with anecdotes about my careers and travels and fears and foibles and friendships.

It was a joyful transition for me, and it has shown me the boundless difference between the drudgery when writing is a chore, and when it's an ever-fresh journey that you long to share with others.

Another reason it was such a happy change was that I found myself working in parallel with my wife's own memoir. Of course, Solange was way ahead of me, not only in text and photographs, but in learning the mysterious ins and outs of dealing with a publisher. Her wonderful autobiography, *No More Tiaras*, has been in bookstores well over a year now, and is prospering. Cheers! And of course, for me and my text, and my frequent need for counsel, Solange has been at my side with answers and judgment, as well as her love.

Finally, a word about my wordy friend, Ron Holland, without whom this memoir would never have gotten off the ground. I met him through his work with Solange…he served as her right-hand man as she brought *No More Tiaras* to life. His presence at our apartment (Solange worked entirely at home) was a joy not only to her, but to me as well. Professionally, Ron has had a long career in advertising, and with his partner, the legendary George Lois, set about turning Madison Avenue upside down. Lately, he's turned his hand to editing novels and biographies, enjoying this literary career as much as his financial one.

Ron's humor is contagious, and his acumen about text structure and word usage is remarkable. Often, as I watched him and Solange working together, I realized not only how much they accomplished, but what fun they had doing so. So naturally, when I began to think seriously about my own memoir, I didn't think twice about asking Ron for a hand. His help has been more than generous, contributing as he always does both a critical eye and a daily dose of laughter and friendship. He tempers his editing pencil with restraint and delicacy, subtly adding coherence to the story line, but always taking care to preserve my Herter voice.

That I now append his name to mine in authoring *May I Cut In?* is not only justified, but brings much happiness to this quarter. Others deserve note for their support, but a special thanks to my daughter, Brooke, who, after reading several early chapters shortly after their inception, thought that my autobiographical task was worthy of continuation. Bless her!

Chris and Fred planning a cavalry chanrge

Chris and Fred, still planning

Charles Pratt (in the white suit) surrounded by progeny, including Fred's grandparents (circled)

CHAPTER ONE

What Hath Great-Grandpa Pratt Wrought?

(A $100 Investment becomes a $300,000,000 Payoff. A Dynasty is Born and Endures. The Pratt Institute is Founded.)

I was born on November 12, 1920, in Brooklyn, New York. Why Brooklyn, you say?

Well, first of all, because I wanted to be close to my mother. But secondly, because of Charles Pratt. He was my great-grandfather on my mother's side. He came from a modest family in Watertown, Massachusetts, but ended up a long, long way from there. His father was the last in a long line of Pratt cabinet makers (genetic echoes of which still flare up in my life-long compulsion to work with my hands, mostly as a surgeon, but with a sideline of home-made, hand-made tables, chairs, and other furniture.) But my great-great-grandmother was the real wonder-worker. Over six long years, she amassed the munificent sum of one hundred dollars, which she gave to 18-year-old Charlie to launch him into the wide world of commerce right after high school.

Backed with this handsome stake, Charles joined a company on the Boston waterfront. Its products were all the by-products of Boston's whaling fleet. A quick study, he learned all the ropes and moved to Brooklyn, New York, setting up Pratt Astral Oil. This fast-growing company supplied America with the different whale oils that illuminated it domestically, and lubricated it industrially.

But then, in a series of 1859 gushers, petroleum erupted throughout western Pennsylvania, making whale oil obsolete almost overnight. My far-thinking forbear immediately added petroleum to the product line of Pratt Astral Oil. He built a refinery in Greenpoint, Brooklyn, then he recruited Henry H. Rogers, and their rapid success at Charles Pratt and Company soon attracted the voracious eye of John D. Rockefeller and his infant Standard Oil Company. One happy day in 1874, the prim figure of John D. appeared at Charles Pratt's door and intoned:

"Mr. Pratt. I'm here to buy you out. I can do that in two different ways: I can either pay you $100,000 right here on the spot. Or I can give you the equivalent stock in Standard Oil of New Jersey. Think about it."

My great-grandfather paced the floor for three days, agonizing over Rockefeller's offer, and then, bless his bones, made the right decision.

Rockefeller quickly made Charles Pratt and Henry Rogers officers at Standard Oil, where their experience and decisiveness boosted Standard Oil in its spectacular growth of a full 1000% from 1874 to 1891, creating for my great- grandfather an appropriate fortune. (Somehow the delightful figure of $300,000,000 comes to mind). And he was not only good at making millions, but also, notably, as a family progenitor, siring a total of eight children. Two from his first wife, and on her death, and after marrying her sister, continuing the line with six more offspring, the first of whom was my grandfather and namesake, Frederic Bayley Pratt, whose three children included the beautiful Mary Caroline, my mother.

Meanwhile, the original Charles Pratt was pondering what to do with his vast riches. One thing for sure, he wanted to keep his family intact down the generations. With that in mind he bought a 2,000-acre property in Glen Cove, Long Island, much of it on the Sound, and about three times the size of Central Park. Then, hiring top-flight architects, and sparing no expense, he built extravagant mansions for five of the last six children he had with his second wife. (The exception, a daughter, was hardly left homeless. She married well to the name and money of one of Boston's finest, Edward P. Dane.) As part of the Pratt compound in Glen Cove, there was a common garage, a horse barn, swimming pools, and even a mausoleum for the Pratt family. The entire enclave sprang from the talents of the Olmstead Brothers who, in their spare time, created the timeless delights of New York's Central Park. The mansion built for my grandfather Frederic and his wife Caroline, whom we called Drachi, had spectacular grounds (thanks to the boundless landscaping genius of the Olmsteads) and a breathtaking view of Long Island Sound. As children living in relatively crowded Boston, we thought the Christmas pilgrimage to the gorgeous expanses of Dosoris Lane in Glen Cove was the high point of our year.

To keep the architects and landscapers hopping, great-grandfather Pratt also built an impressive group of houses along Clinton Avenue in Brooklyn, two blocks from the Pratt Institute. 232 Clinton Avenue was the mansion Charles built for himself in 1887, with four children's abodes clustered about him. The largest of which, at 229 Clinton, fell to my grandfather, Frederic Pratt. It was there I made my first appearance to this world. But I lived there for only 3 months, leaving for Washington D.C., where my father, Christian Herter, then held his first diplomatic post. Not for 35 years did I return to my birthplace, which is now Pratt Institute's president's house. All the magnificent homes my great-grandfather built eventually coalesced to create the campus of Pratt Institute. Among its other distinctions is the Pratt Free Library, America's first public library. So it's no coincidence that Pratt boasts the oldest School of Library Science in the country.

I must add one relevant story –how our Pratt grandparents met in New York while they were both teenagers. He, Fred, fell for Caroline at first sight. Now in all frankness, that's a little hard to believe because even in those days the camera did not lie, and her early photographs have preserved a maiden who was far from pretty. Nevertheless, when she left to go back to her home in Oregon, he swore to join her there to plight his boyish troth. But friends and family warned him of the dangers of cross-country train travel. (The Wild West wasn't for the faint-hearted in the late 1800's).

"Good God, Fred! Haven't you heard of the Indian uprisings in the Great Plains?"

With this lucky tip, he took a boat around South America and up the West Coast. A full three-month trip, at least. But a success! He won his bride and saved his scalp.

It would be unfair to dismiss my Great-Grandfather Charles as a parvenu for his ostentatious displays of wealth or even to brand him a "Robber Baron" for the way he amassed it. He was anything but. Money was not the god he worshipped. That's why he established and supported a Baptist church in Brooklyn. And that's also why he spent much of his life (and a great deal of his fortune) supporting the needy and educating the unschooled. The Pratt Free Library (America's first) was his creation, but the act that has kept his name in the public eye right up to the present day was his founding of the Pratt Institute, revolutionizing the very concept of a vocational school. Starting with only fifteen students, like Topsy, it just grew into today's burgeoning liberal arts institution with over four thousand gifted students. There they become skilled in creative writing, architecture, interior and industrial design, commercial art, fine arts, information and library science, and urban design and planning. Charles Pratt described his dream very simply, in powerful egalitarian prose:

"I wish to found a school that shall help all classes of workers, artists, artisans, apprentices and homemakers, and I wish its courses conducted in such a way as to give every student practical skill along some definite line of work, and at the same time reveal to him possibilities for further development and study."

A year after Pratt Institute opened; Charles Pratt spoke again, on Founder's Day, October 2, 1888. And as always, his simple, lively words are fresh and relevant today. Listen:

"It is my earnest desire that Pratt graduates 60 strong, helpful, sincere men and women prepared to do efficient work, and remain unwilling to do less than their best. I wish I could convince you of the belief I have in the power of the life and purpose of a young man or woman, and the influence they may have for good in this world. It is right here from you that I look for the success of the Institute. I believe in the spirit of fellowship, in that unity of thought and action which tends to make others even better. Don't go through life finding fault. Instead, try to find the strong points in those around you and help make the world better and brighter. All pleasure in life comes from helping others. That is the reason I built this Institute. Busy people are happy people. So keep busy. Honest effort will make work a pleasure, and overcome all difficulties. Working for the genuine and true will sweeten and give courage to life."

He himself never had a day of advanced schooling, but he made up for that omission by sending five of his six sons to Amherst College. My grandfather, Frederic, was the Pratt Institute's president for thirty years, and he was followed in that post by my uncle, Charles Pratt, and then by a cousin, Jerry Pratt. Today, Mitchell Pratt, my first cousin once removed, is Chairman of the Pratt Institute's Board of Trustees. (As you can see, my family may have a few faults, but nepotism is certainly not among them.) I guess this is a good time to extend the family's eternal thanks to the father of our tribe, Charles Pratt. Not a day passes that I don't send a nod of appreciation in his direction.

My mother, Mary Caroline, (May Carrie to family, 'Mac' to friends), attended the Packer Institute in Brooklyn and then moved to a girl's finishing school in Connecticut called Farmington (or more formally, Miss Porter's). Her closest friend there was Caroline Keck, and the love of that Caroline's life was Everit Herter, my father's older brother. That's how my father happened to join Everit on a weekend at Miss Porter's, and how he met my mother. This fortuitous meeting of Christian Herter and his beloved 'Mac' led to their marriage in Glen Cove, Long Island, in 1917.

Portrait of Charles Pratt, to whom the enducational world owes much and more

Father called on to serve as Secretary of the Paris Peace Commission in Versailles

Frederic Pratt and his grandchildren, including Chris and me (circled)

My ever-serious, ever-handsome father Christian Herter

12

Couldn't you guess? It's Gammy!

The modest homes built for Charles and his children in Brooklyn

Sixty-Second Edition of

THE WHOLE PRATT WORKS

CHARLES PRATT
October 2, 1830 - May 4, 1891

Lydia Ann
Richardson
December 13, 1835
- August 5, 1861

Mary Helen
Richardson
January 31, 1839
- January 20, 1907

A book on the Pratt family before its connection to John D.

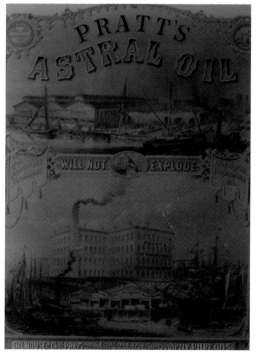

PRATT'S
ASTRAL OIL

WILL NOT EXPLODE

Charles Pratt's beginnings in Brooklyn, where Astral Oil was born

The Pratt family's rapid transportation!

Drachi, my beautiful (to me) grandmother

The site of my 1st and 90th birthdays

Daddy long-legs   *...As you can see, they run in the family*

CHAPTER TWO

MY FATHER, BORN
TWO CENTURIES AGO

(An Unhappy Paris Childhood. Blooming at Harvard, with
First Rungs on a Sky-high Career.)

My father, Christian Archibald Herter, was born in 1895. Much of his childhood was spent in Paris where his parents were studying at the Ecole des Beaux Arts. From age six and on he attended the Ecole Alsacienne. The school's accelerated curriculum gave him a three-year advantage over his American colleagues. Which is why he could enter Harvard at the ripe old age of sixteen! The years between the Ecole Alsatienne and Harvard were spent at the progressive Browning School in New York. Just to keep it all in the family, Browning's headmaster was an old friend of my Dad's father, Albert Herter.

This wasn't a happy period for my father. His parents were still in Paris, so he was forced to live in New York with his uncle, Christian Archibald Herter, an uptight, humorless Germanic doctor. This martinet was so fanatically disciplined he demanded that each bedtime, my father compile a written agenda covering every fifteen minutes period, projected for the following day. This for a 12-year-old boy!

But Uncle Arch, as the doctor was called, was probably not the arch-fiend my father made him out to be. Just consider his track record: A brilliant physician, a graduate of Columbia's School of Medicine, a professor of medicine at two universities in New York, author of many texts, he also was a founder of the Rockefeller Institute. The top floor of his Madison Avenue house was entirely devoted to laboratories and to free housing for his students interested in research. (One of the young researchers spending a year on Dr. Herter's top floor was Henry Drysdale Dakin, inventor of Dakin's Solution, an anti-bacterial used extensively during World War 1. This same Dr. Dakin married the widow of my great-grandfather, Christian Augustus Ludwig

Herter, and they lived out their lives in Santa Barbara, California.)

But Uncle Arch's major passion was music and he was gifted on both piano and the strings, especially cello. It's really humbling to think of all this remarkable man accomplished before he died at only forty-four of an undiagnosed illness.

I can add one personal note about Uncle Arch. Many years ago I operated on a young woman from New Jersey. When she heard my name she asked if I could possibly be related to a Dr. Christian Herter who once lived on Madison Avenue?

"Yes, I am. But why do you ask?"

"Well, because my grandfather, as a child, took violin lessons on Madison Avenue. One day a Dr. Herter stopped the boy and asked why he was lugging a violin case almost larger than he. A long conversation went on to include the boy's parents, and ended with Uncle Arch offering to assume the cost of the boy's entire musical education.

To my delight, this charming patient of mine invited me to Carnegie Hall shortly thereafter to hear her 83-year-old grandfather's last solo violin concert. His well-known name was Joseph Fuchs, and his final concert still plays in my memory. When we met backstage after the performance, there were embraces and tears and laughter and it was wonderful.

In the interest of full disclosure, I should add this thought. I'll bet my father's dislike of Uncle Arch stemmed from my father's being chosen, rather than his older brother Everit, to complete his schooling in New York, instead of Paris. I also can't help wondering, as I sit here sifting through my memories, if this wasn't also the reason my father didn't take too kindly to my choice of medicine as a career.

My father, Christian Herter, graduated from Harvard a year after his brother Everit. It was 1915, and Dad was only 19. He was a bright, if not overly industrious, student. The best mark he had in his first two years was a B, but somehow he wound up with a cum laude degree. And he had extracurricular triumphs, to boot. He was President of the Signet Society (literature, debating), an officer of the Spee Club, and played competitive tennis. But he was still uncertain about his future. Many in the Herter family were artistically gifted. My father's grandfather, Christian Augustus Ludwig Herter was a prime example. He left Stuttgart, Germany in 1859 to join his older half brother, Julius Gustave Alexander Hagenlacher, an established interior decorator in New York. He had spent some of his earlier life in the Ecole des Beaux Arts in Paris, and his consuming desire was to return to Paris to take up painting once again. Painting was clearly his first love. But he was driven by family responsibilities, and his joining Gustave was the key to making Herter Brothers so wildly successful.

They won commissions to design, fit out, and decorate such plums as the Governor Latham mansion, along with those of Mark Hopkins, D.O. Mills, William H. Vanderbilt, Jr., Pierpont Morgan, H.R. Bishop and other buildings in the public eye. They employed over 100 German artisans and brought them to New York, to design and build Herter Brothers furniture locally. Herter Brothers rapidly became the most fashionable decorative mark of the era.

And the reason for that success must go principally to Christian, whose artistic talents swiftly outshone Gustave's. "Each assignment bears the stamp of Christian Herter's rare, vigorous, and brilliant mind," his biography quotes.

This friend of Emerson and Thoreau made up his mind to earn one million dollars, and then leave Herter Brothers for Paris, where he was going to start painting again. This he did by the time he was thirty-eight years old. So he pulled up stakes, and went to Paris, leaving his family behind in New York. But he had only four short years of acting out his painterly dream. He died in 1883 of some then undiagnosed disease, perhaps consumption or a neurological dysfunction. It presaged the early death of his son, Dr. Christian Archibald Herter, 32 years later, once again of an unknown cause.

Ironically, in the strange way the world turns, his paintings never gained notoriety. But ten years ago, the Metropolitan Museum of Art gave a successful show starring the work of... the Herter Brothers! But their fame rested not on their paintings, but on their striking interior decorations.

It's hard to believe that today no one in my family owns a single piece of Herter Brothers furniture. In fact, I had never heard of this famous pair until one day in the 1950's when a graduate student called me and asked if she could see some of my Herter Brothers furniture collection!

My grandfather Albert Marsh Herter (Gampy) and our grandmother Adele McGinnis Herter, (Gammy), were painters of note. They met each other while studying art in Paris. Her father was a well-known politician who rose to become Governor of New York. These two young artists soon became more than friends. They began married life painting their way through Japan. Then they resumed their studies in Paris at the Ecole des Beaux Arts.

Gampy's skill as a draftsman began when he was a boy. When he was 16, he sold his first painting, a life-size nude. And talk about luck, decades later my father found it hanging behind a bar in an Albany club! I never asked how my father happened to be in that bar, but he was delighted to have located the nude, which his father had long ago described to him. I suspect...no, I hope, that alluring nude still tempts imbibers from behind that bar to this day.

Only recently, as I walked past the glass door to the Spanier Gallery in Manhattan, I glimpsed a life-size painting of a young girl in white. I was struck by its beauty, all the more so when I stepped inside and found out the painting was by Albert Herter, in 1891. So this was done when my grandfather was twenty, and was on sale for $950,000! And Gampy's taste, (pre-Gammy) in toothsome young things was worth at least that!

Another important portrait he did was of his two sons, Everit and my father, Christian Herter. The boys were sitting back-to-back on a sofa, a pillow between their heads, and reading.. It was acquired by the Metropolitan Museum and for year after year won the prize for being the most popular painting at the Museum. To get the painting back to the family Gampy had to donate several lesser paintings from his own collection to the Met. (It's now owned by my brother Miles and hangs in his house in Manchester, Mass.)

Here's another story about Gampy. Once while working in his Paris studio, his phone rang. The call was from John D. Rockefeller, an old acquaintance from New York. He was in Paris, and wondered if he might visit the studio.

"Of course, John," Gampy said, "but I'll be working until late afternoon, and will welcome you then."

My grandfather was well aware that John D. was an incorrigible prude, and on an easel in the studio was a nearly completed painting of a voluptuous nude model, who was still sitting there, in the flesh. Gampy immediately added a not-quite diaphanous undergarment to the canvas, to protect the world's richest man from impure thought. He also asked the model to dress and sit quietly by during the visit. John D. arrived, sat on a sofa facing the painting, nodded his approval and the visit began. They chattered on, 15 minutes became an hour, and the model became bored out of her mind. So she decided to terminate the interview. She shed all her clothes, stood on her hands, and walked on her hands directly in front of Rockefeller. And that's the moment she let her legs fall apart. "Sacre Bleu!" Or maybe "Goodness gracious!" escaped John D.'s puritanical lips. And I'm not sure if the Herter and Rockefeller friendship cooled to non-existence, or actually increased, from that delightful moment. But Gampy sure loved telling that story, over and over.

Gampy Herter is remembered even today for his splendid murals, which capture significant segments of American history. They adorn the central assembly rooms of statehouses in Connecticut, Wisconsin, Nebraska and of course, Boston. The murals in Massachusetts were presented while my father was its Governor. Other murals were seen in New York's Grand Central Station, at Wellesley College, at the Public Library in Los Angeles, and in two grand hotels in San Francisco.

But Albert Herter remains best known for his enormous mural at the Gare de L'Est in Paris, immortalizing the French troops boarding the trains heading for the front in World War I. It was commissioned by the French government shortly after the war's end and an entire wing at Versailles was provided Gampy as a studio. After the epic mural was completed in 1926, it was hoisted into place above the train entrance at the Gare de L'Est. Its unveiling was an historic occasion, culminated by my grandfather receiving the familiar red lapel-ribbon of the Chevalier de la Legion d'Honneur. The medal was presented by Marshal Joffre.

It was a particularly bittersweet event for the Herter family. Everit, my father's brother, had been killed in action during the last days of that war-to-end-all-wars. Everit was a distinguished artist in his own right, a joyful and charming young man, greatly beloved by his brother and perhaps even more so by his mother. She claimed that she knew precisely the date and time of day of his death. This apparent clairvoyance led to her involvement with spiritualism, and she spent much of her life thereafter attending séances as she tried to connect with her son. This never happened, couldn't happen, but Everit's death remained a doleful part of her daily existence.

Everit was in the Camouflage Corps, very appropriate when you consider his reputation as an artist. He was killed on the same day my father was taking his entrance exams for diplomacy at the Department of State, in Washington. Also on the day Everit died, Dwight Bridges, a fellow artist in the Camouflage Corps, was trying to find him on the battlefield to award him his lieutenant's bars, making him an officer. That meeting never took place. (Much later, Dwight married Everit's widow, Caroline Keck.)

Whenever you're in Paris, this mural is worthy of a visit. In addition to the train of departing troops you can pick out a dimly illumined Everit peering through a train window sadly viewing this family on the platform below him, a small huddle of Albert Herter, holding the hand of Everit's six-year-old son, and beside him the boy's mother, Caroline Keck, Everit's wife. When I first saw the mural in 1931, I was astounded by the number of people around me, some of them weeping. And two years ago, when I returned to the Gare de l'est for still another poignant look, the tears were largely mine, but the viewers, standing silently about me in sad reflection, all these years (and wars) later, were surprising in number.

Back to the present: Recently, on October 15, 2011, during a short vacation in Paris, I visited the mural for the 4th or 5th time. It's magic for me was unchanged. While I was photographing the scene, my wife, Solange, fell into a conversation with two elderly souls sitting nearby, apparently taken by the mural. "Are you familiar with the painting?, Solange asked. "Heavens yes," came the reply, in French "Albert Herter was asked by the French to do the mural. This was after they learned that his son, Everit, had been killed in the last days of the war. They even provided Albert a wing at Versailles, to do the work. It was completed in 1926."

This couple was as delighted as I was to meet at the Gare de L'est almost 90 years later.

One last note about my Herter grandparents: After Everit and Christian were born, they had one more child, Lydia. When she was three, Lydia developed encephalitis and almost died. Her survival was a mixed blessing. Although brilliant in math and the sciences, she found many areas of life, especially social skills, very tough going. To get along, she had to share her life with a companion, Ingaborg Praetorius, a guardian and friend. Much of their life was spent in Santa Barbara, at El Mirasol, the extraordinary house built by Mary Miles Herter, my grandfather Gampy's mother. El Mirasol was an unbelievably sumptuous dwelling, set in an entire city block. Lydia, disabilities and all, was included in as many of the family doings as possible, and spent nearly her entire life there. She died in 1951.

Wouldn't you think that after my father graduated from Harvard he would have chosen some artistic direction to guide his life? Well, so he did. Architecture. But his short architectural schooling in Cambridge ended abruptly when his closest friend, Lithgow Osborne, offered him a job at the American embassy in Berlin, headed by Ambassador Joseph Grew. Lithgow's father, Thomas Mott Osborne, was the brilliant penologist who drastically overhauled the design and purpose of prisons in New York. Young Lithgow was editor of the only liberal newspaper in upper New York State. And it remains so today, in Auburn, under the directorship of Lithgow's son, Eric.

Father came to know Lithgow during their freshman year at Harvard, and that summer he visited the Osborne family in their Northeast Harbor home in Maine. That vacation trip had lifelong reverberations. Because on the first Sunday, Father accompanied the Osbornes to their usual worship at the Episcopalian Church. This was a new experience for him, as his own family was irreligious, and I doubt he'd ever been inside a church before. He was introduced to the pastor, who greeted him by asking what and where his parish was?

My father replied, "Why, I don't even know what a parish is."

"Well, in that case," said the kindly minister, "You're not welcome in this church."

Because of this unbelievably callous comment, my father remained a church abstainer throughout his life. But he was also a pragmatic politician in a heavily Catholic Boston community, so he finally gave in, and at the age of thirty-six he faced the baptismal font, along with his four children, at Boston's Trinity Church. The spiritual aspects of the baptismal rite was somewhat diluted by the disappearance of 3-year-old Miles among the pews. (You can imagine my delight when I went to see the Broadway hit, Life With Father, and one scene had Clarence Day heading off to church. A neighbor yelled, "Where you off to, Clarence?' And he answers, "To be baptized, Goddammit!")

But back to my father, receiving that intriguing invitation from Lithgow

Osborne, to join him in the Foreign Service. On the spot, he abandoned architecture and took the next boat eastward. His experience in Berlin as it turned out, was short and sweet. Ambassador Grew dispatched him almost immediately to the U.S. Embassy in Brussels, where there was greater need. But his stay there was also brief. America by then was about to declare war. So father came home and tried to enlist in the Army. But towering 6 feet five inches, and weighing 135 pounds soaking wet, he was laughed out of the enlistment hall. After all, they couldn't make up a special uniform for just one beanpole private! (I should add that his spindly physical make-up was especially severe in childhood. Indeed, he had to wear hip-high steel leg braces for six years until he was nine.)

So off to Washington my father went. But not before taking time to wed Mary Caroline Pratt. The wedding took place in 1917, at the Frederic Pratt house in Glen Cove. It was an elaborate and happy affair (just look at the photographs). My father took his bride to the Waldorf for the night, armed with a $100 dollar bill, but at checkout time the next day he could find only one dollar in his wallet. (Apparently a lucky taxi driver got a colossal tip!) At any rate, his friend Osborne had to bail them out of their honeymoon hotel! A memorable beginning to any marriage. Then, almost immediately, duty called. America had entered the war.

The State Department named Father a Special Assistant, in charge of creating a prisoner-of-war agreement with Germany in 1918. While visiting prison camps, he noted that many of the inmates wore red bands on their arms, declaring themselves Communists. Starvation was endemic. The State Department next suggested that father consult with his old friend from Berlin, Kurt Hahn*, to learn how to answer the growing Communist influence, using food. This led to Washington sending $350,000,000 worth of foodstuffs. Dad used these provisions to solve both problems: first, starvation, then, Communism. On the heels of this, Secretary of State Robert Lansing called on father to serve as Secretary to the Paris Peace Commission in Versailles the next year he was named Special Assistant to Herbert Hoover, and had an active role on the European Relief Council. In 1921 Hoover became Secretary of Commerce and my father's final foreign job was directing the Hoover Commission's task of combating widespread starvation in Southern Russia.

*Kurt Hahn: celebrated for the Secondary Schools he created, daily high-jumping as mandatory as the 3 R's. In Hahn's Scotland's Gordenston School, one of Hahn's creations, Prince Charles endured icy showers and lackluster food to build character. I guess it worked. In America, the Outward Bound schools were Hahn's most successful creations, and they remain so today.

My father's brother, Everit, K.I.A. on the last day of World War I

Friends in Millis, Mass.

My father and his brother Everit, captured by Gampy

Me and my brother Chris, captured by Mir

CHAPTER THREE

HERBERT HOOVER'S LAP, AT 2, AND OTHER EARLY MEMORIES

(Fun and Frights in D.C. and Boston. Mir, a Perfect Stranger, Joins the Family, Thanks to Mother, and Becomes my Perfect Godmother. "I'm Three!")

I had moved from Brooklyn to Washington when I was only three months old, so I had no first hand knowledge of my father's activities in Foreign Affairs during that critical period, but by 1922, as a two year old, I was on the scene in Washington and remember sitting on Mr. Hoover's lap as the grown-ups had cocktails before dinner.

Many years later, someone asked me what my earliest memories were. I could think of only of two things aside from President Hoover:

The first memory was being wakened in my crib in Washington and encountering a wicked witch replete with broomstick and hat. I wish I could claim that I calmly asked "Who are you?" but instead I gave a scream, and the witch confessed to being a local fireman. And what perfect timing, because I next heard my mother yelling for someone to put out a blaze in the kitchen!

My other remembrance, perhaps even clearer, came from Boston, where we moved in 1923. We lived at 9 Chestnut Street on Beacon Hill, and on my birthday, November 12th of that year, my mother arranged a party. My older brother Chris and I sat at either end of the dining room table, and between us there was a gang of our small-fry friends. Somehow the importance of the event took over and I remember standing up on the chair and shouting across the table to my brother:

"Chris, I'm three, I'm three!" Somehow it never crossed my mind that a short 87 years later I'd reach my present age of 90. An associated memory of that day – we had ice cream for dessert...all we wanted...and each frozen treat was molded into a fascinating shape. Mine, I remember, was a perfectly detailed model of a chocolate submarine.

Oh yes! There was another event in Washington, one that had a major effect on my life.

One day, as my mother was strolling home through Montrose Park, she came upon a young woman on a bench, weeping her heart out. Mother, with typical kindness, sat down and engaged the forlorn creature in sympathetic conversation. She sobbed out her story:

Back in Vienna, the famous Doctor Pirquet, an expert in tuberculosis, had adopted her. Her name was Margaret Fisher and I learned much later that she was the illegitimate daughter of Parquet's brother. She had accompanied Dr. Pirquet on a cross-America lecture tour that ended in D.C. There, out of the blue, Pirquet had become acutely depressed and had flung himself from the tenth floor of the Mayflower Hotel. This had happened three days before.

She sat there, slumped, and continued to cry,

"I don't know what to do or where to go." And my mother quickly set her straight.

"Well, I know what you're going to do; you're coming home with me". So they walked home, arm in arm, and Mir, as she came to be called, stayed with us for the next ten years. She not only became nurse to my older brother and me, but was much more like our surrogate mother. One summer morning when I was seven, I awoke to find my genitals so swollen they were unrecognizable. I was almost too scared to look at them, but didn't know whom I should show them to, Mother or Mir? There were no other options. My brother Chris was away, and my little friends would probably be jealous. Well, I'll bet you already guessed, after an hour of agonizing and pondering, I chose Mir. She looked and laughed and made the diagnosis: Poison Ivy! So my guilt at not having chosen mother swiftly evaporated. Mir was totally engaging, bright; lovely looking and she spoke five languages fluently. Most importantly, she became not only my mother's closest friend, but my godmother, too. (A good many years later I asked her if she'd become godmother to my oldest child, Eric, and of course she leapt at the chance.)

Mir finally moved back to Vienna, where she rejoined her by then ancient mother, and later married a World War I veteran named Otto Papesch. Otto was being enticed to enroll again, this time in Hitler's army. He refused, at least for a time, and they lived happily in Nussdorf, a lovely village on the Danube, close to Vienna. We visited them there twice (mother, Chris and I) and had joyous Falt boat trips down the river to Vienna from the German border.

But Mir wanted to have children and Otto didn't. She finally threatened to leave him unless he relented. This he did, and in time two children, a boy and a girl, were born to them. But this new war intervened, cruelly, as always. While on the Polish front, Otto developed tuberculosis, and was sent home, and died surrounded by family. But Mir was left with two young children to raise, so she fell back on her native language skills and became a well-known translator. She was a favorite with many embassies in Europe and some commercial firms, too. She did well enough to send her son, Peter, to Harvard, and Gingi, her daughter, to Radcliff. They also did well for themselves. Peter became an architect and real estate developer in Cambridge, and Gingi now lives happily with her children in Australia. And three years ago, to my whole family's astonishment and delight, Peter made a generous gift to Harvard, which established the Christian Herter Chair in Government.

So you can see that Mir was in every sense a part of our family, an important part, and a year never passed without exchange visits between her and our family. She outlived Mother by several years, but Chris and I went to her funeral in Vienna when she died, at the age of 95. How lucky we were to have had her with us, particularly during our growing years, and we still bless Mother for having brought that luckless waif home that lucky day.

Chris and Fred

Our Family

Fred and his mother, on the Danube

Mir, surrounded by family and friends in Vienna

Fred and Chris, into mischief

With Mother and Mir, falt-boating on the Danube. I'm in the glam shades!

31

The great Christian Archibald Herter, Patriot

FATHER'S POLITICAL CAREER, WITH NEVER AN ELECTION LOST

(13 years in the Massachusetts House of Representatives.
5 Terms in U.S. Congress. Implementation of the Marshall Plan.
Social Education of Richard Nixon.)

But back to Washington in 1923, still as Hoover's assistant, Father had to make some difficult decisions. For five years he'd been heavily involved in foreign affairs and now felt it was time to lay this aside. A close friend from Boston, Richard Danielson, invited him to help publish a new magazine of politics and economics. It was to be called The Independent. So our family moved to Boston, and The Independent was launched. Alas, it was a little too academic for the public, never built a substantial circulation, and lasted only three years. But my father's articles made clear his strong support for the League of Nations. He was a staunch critic of isolationism and spent 1929-1930 at Harvard, lecturing on behalf of the League.

Danielson then proposed a new "slick" magazine, *The Sportsman.* It was intended to replace *The Independent* and maybe have a happier reception by the public. It was large. It was slick. But it cost a whopping 50 cents. That half-dollar cover price was a killer during the Great Depression. My father wrote some material for it and served as editor, but it was clear that his future did not lie in magazines. So, with our breadwinner once again unemployed, we found ourselves at 9 Chestnut Street on Beacon Hill in Boston. At age three, I entered a school called Little Beaver, within view of the Charles River Basin, and my education began.

At the same time, Father began his elective political career. A friend talked him into running for the Massachusetts House of Representatives. He won that election and held his seat for 13 years, the last three as Speaker of the House. In 1942, he ran for Congress in Washington and served there for five full terms. His proudest post in Congress was as chairman of the 19-member committee to implement the Marshall Plan for Europe. The committee spent a full month of unrelenting work in Europe, and the most industrious and effective member of his committee (and I know this sounds strange), Richard Milhous Nixon! But, Nixon or not, the work of the Marshall Plan Committee remains unmatched in effectively changing the world.

Here's a telling aside about Nixon:

During the course of Marshall Plan activities, Nixon became friendly with Philip Watts, the well-born, Harvard educated and socially prominent manager of the committee's agenda. You couldn't possibly put together two more poles-apart people, in terms of economic, social or family background. Nixon was uneasy, to the point of paranoia, in trying to understand the ways of the Ivy League, and was incapable of attaining for himself the socially comfortable and interlocking friendships of the northeastern elite. That's why Phil Watts, an urbane and self-confident blue-blood, was the perfect mentor for Nixon to call on for advice on how to behave, how to comport himself at formal events, what clothes to wear, how to address new acquaintances, what drinks to order (What is a Martini, anyway?). If I exaggerate his dread of social gaffes, or his awareness of the enormous social gulf between the mentor and the student, it's not by much. The man was almost pathologically uncomfortable in his own skin. Still today, isn't it sad to think of Nixon, even after he reached the matchless heights of the Presidency, still calling on Phil for advice on how to handle himself during yet another social event in the White House. And faithful Phil was always obliging.

Though Father always denied any interest in moving back to Boston after his ten years in Washington, he reluctantly accepted the Republican candidacy for governor of Massachusetts. He won in a cliffhanger in 1952 but handily in 1954. By then, I was far from the political scene in Massachusetts, but I knew, from family and every other quarter, that he was a strong and popular Governor.

In 1956, Dad triumphantly returned to Washington as Dwight D. Eisenhower's Under Secretary of State. That election year found him prominent in the news as a possible candidate for the Presidency. Harold Stassen was his prime supporter, but the candidacy was wrongly thought to be illegal because of Father's birth in Paris. As things turned out, and as proof of his loyal Republicanism, he gave the speech at the Convention nominating Nixon as the Vice-Presidential candidate. Two years later he was elevated to Secretary of State, and when JFK replaced Ike, father resigned and remained in the Capital as Chief Trade Administrator for both Kennedy and Johnson with the title of Ambassador. Father's death in 1966 was premature – he was only 71.

What do I most remember about my father? Many, many things, but most of all, his courage. From early middle age, arthritis, with its ever-increasing pain, forced him to give up the outdoor sports he loved; tennis, golf, and finally hunting, in that order. Eventually, this fine-postured man could get around only with arm-crutches. But I don't think I ever, not even once, heard him complain. But how I remember his promising response when he was admitted to Presbyterian Hospital for trial treatment with the latest wonder drug: the steroid Prednisone. I visited him a few hours after his first injection, and I'd never before seen him so excited!

"Watch this, Fred!" and he jumped out of bed, strode across the room, and stood ramrod straight, back against the wall. And not for just a moment, but easily for a full minute. A feat I could barely duplicate myself. But this near-miraculous release from pain, and his ecstatic joy, were short lived. The side effects of the steroids were so serious that he could take them only in extreme circumstances. He left the hospital a deeply saddened man. (I've often pondered since then whether his remaining years would have been less painful had he never tasted that fleeting rapture of total pain relief, and, for a few blissful days, the joy of unrestricted physical activity.)

Father suffered other serious problems. His life-long smoking habit led to emphysema, and even worse, COPD, or chronic obstructive pulmonary disease. While being hospitalized for this, at Presbyterian Hospital in New York, his unrecognized aortic aneurysm ruptured. This required an emergency aortic replacement, which allowed him to live for another ten years. (I still bless Arthur Voorhees for his skills as a vascular surgeon.)

When reminiscing about my father, I remember how the people he lived and worked with, without exception, brought up his invincible integrity. He simply did not know the meaning of dishonesty or evasion of the truth. His utter dependability was the reason President Eisenhower turned to him first when seeking advice about the thorny issues confronting his administration. Ike also valued my father's unblemished code of personal behavior.

As Arthur Krock, the great New York Times reporter recalled in his 'Memoirs': "...in the middle of a cabinet meeting, John J. McCloy, the Chairman of the Atomic Energy Commission, was arguing for his point of view on dealing with American and Russian inspection systems. Finally, an exasperated President Eisenhower pounded his desk and said:

"I intend to follow Christian Herter's counsel in these ventures. Period!"

When he was Governor of Massachusetts, his State House followers also depended deeply on Father's judgment. I remember speaking to many of them when they invaded New York's Plaza Hotel to watch Rocky Marciano defend his Heavyweight Championship in Yankee Stadium. These were rough-edged, street-smart political pros, and I was astonished at their unanimity in applying these somewhat formal adjectives to Dad's work.

"He has great judgment!"

"He was almost never wrong about people...or issues."

"He never wavered or went back on his word."

"He was simply great!"

And I was simply proud. Who wouldn't be?

I should add that Dad's gubernatorial work was occasionally brightened by a pre-luncheon martini in the State House dining room. One such lunch found him exchanging political banter with his colleagues. Dad was focusing on the upcoming Senatorial battle between Henry Cabot Lodge (a Boston Brahman, if there ever was one), and James Michael Curley, the Mayor of Boston, popular even though he spent part of his term in jail! My father's political career in Boston inevitably brought him into face-offs with Mayor Curley. But their confrontations were never really adversarial. Strange as it seems, these two opposing warriors kind of liked each other, all their disparities aside.

But back to that political lunch. Dad suddenly offered a shocking wager:

"I'll bet anyone 5000 bucks that Lodge will whomp Curley by over 300,000 votes!"

In the shocked silence that followed, a gnarled finger tapped Dad's shoulder, and turning, he saw none other than Hizzoner James M. Curley, taking five crisp thousand-dollar bills out of his wallet, and plunking them down in front of my father.

Happily (and luckily) Lodge trounced Curley by well over those 300,000 votes.

While in Washington, Father initiated several organizations that influenced America's foreign service. The most important was SAIS (School of Advanced International Studies). He and Paul Nitze (who married my mother's first cousin) founded SAIS in 1943, and it was eventually absorbed by Johns Hopkins University. It has evolved into the best training center for Foreign Service professionals and has branches in Bologna, Italy and Nanjing, China. (My brother Chris taught there in his later years.)

In 1947, Dad set up the Middle East Institute, with the scholar George Earl Keiser. Later that same year this inexhaustible man joined the Board of the World Peace Foundation. Shortly after he died, in 1966, the American Foreign Service Association established the Christian A, Herter Award to honor bold diplomats who challenge the status quo. But probably the acknowledgment he cherished most was the Presidential Medal of Freedom, given him in 1961. Once, when I was thinking of the impressive number of governmental jobs he'd held, I asked him, what single goal do you think counted most in your political career? Christian Herter's answer was swift, emphatic and unforgettable: "Good government."

I'm still in awe that his simple, direct and meaningful answer took only two words. And yet those words encapsulated my father's entire life's work.

Father didn't always display the easy warmth of my mother, or the close touch she had with us children. And his growing public responsibilities meant that we saw little of him. Cheehacombahee, the South Carolina plantation that Grandfather Pratt bought on the eve of the Great Depression (the price was right: 12 thousand dollars for 12 thousand acres), proved to be a perfect setup for bringing the whole family together Mother delighted in spending three or four weeks there in the winter months. Father made it down for no more than two (and we children were lucky to make it for one). It was there, in that absolutely glorious spot abutting the Cheeha and Combahee Rivers, and amidst duck, quail and dove hunts that friendships were born, and love cemented.

Father loved it there, even up to the time when he could no longer ride tall in the saddle, nor follow the bird dogs through the thick woods. His love for this land was transmitted to us. It was only there that he seemed totally relaxed, even happy, with only a detective story or a bridge game, once hunting was beyond his physical ability, and other adventures were available only to us young 'uns. But fortunately we were wise enough in our youth to use that time to close the gaps in our relationships with him. It's still a pleasure to recall his painstaking instructions for the next day's hunt, especially the night-before preparation for early morning duck shoots. Before bedtime we had to lay out our cold-weather clothes, in strict order, starting with underwear, and ending it up with jacket, headgear and gloves. It sounds a little silly, but in the predawn and darkness it made a lot of sense to develop this habit. And oh what joy we found in every aspect of our stays at Cheehacombahee, from the 5am duck shoots to the long horseback rides out to some glorious site for lunch. Then saddling up for an afternoon of quail shooting, followed by a happy ride homeward for a tin tub bath before roaring flames in the bedroom fireplace. Can you imagine how delectable drinks and dinner were to top off such a day? But that wasn't all…dinner was usually followed by charades or bridge or laugh-laden talk. It was heaven to all of us, regardless of age or inclination. Father reveled in it. Those magical days were all too few, alas, but the memories are indelible even decades later.

There was another vacation spot that re-built our relationship with Father. Mountainy Pond, at East Holden, Maine, was a lovely 3-mile-long lake, bounded by mountains. For a few days each summer, the whole family would make it our longed-for goal. There was no electricity. There was no running water. We ate and read by lamplight, and we bathed by leaping into the icy lake. But beyond its physical beauty and the back-to-nature gift it bestowed, what I remember most about Mountainy Pond was its unearthly…silence. It blessed the outdoors with a profound sense of isolation. There must have been a few camps somewhere around us, but we could neither see nor hear them. Exactly one motorboat, the caretaker's, was allowed on the lake, and the single other imposition on the silence was the eerily mystical cry of the loon. The endless days were filled with swimming, long walks through the primeval woods, or bass fishing. And, as from time immemorial, the thoughts of youth were long, long thoughts. Best of all, the manifest happiness of my father at the camp communicated itself to all of us, and I felt blissfully comfortable with him.

I remember very well trying to fell a tree, a small one, maybe, but not to a 7-year-old lumberjack. Swinging my trusty hatchet, I missed the tree, but not my leg and I didn't even cry until I saw all the blood. I still have the vivid memory of Father rowing me the length of the lake, then driving me two hours to Northeast Harbor, and holding my hand as the doctor stitched me up. Because there were no antibiotics in those days, my leg soon became infected. I spent the rest of the summer on the sick list, welcoming the attentions of Mother and Father both. I'm happy to report that the camp at idyllic Mountainy Pond now belongs to my brother, Miles, with the downside that his own four children and infinite number of grandchildren easily fill all the available slots.

As his importance in Washington lessened, I could sense Dad's desire to see us more and make up for the separateness of our early lives. This applied largely to Del, Miles and myself, who, by occupation or geography, were at a distance from P Street in Georgetown. But Chris lived in the neighborhood, so they saw much of each other.

I must tell you now about a special evening in which Father came up to Dobbs Ferry to have dinner with me and Harriet, my second wife and mother of Caroline and Brooke.. This was an uncommon event; he rarely traveled to New York. During dinner I told him about Roosevelt Hospital asking me to leave Presbyterian Hospital to become Director of Surgical Services there. Roosevelt was a fine hospital; indeed, I thought it was the finest clinical (as opposed to academic) center in the city. I knew many of the doctors working at Roosevelt, and the salary was well above what I made at Columbia. Father was unusually attentive during my explanation. But when I told him I had finally declined the offer, he reproached me with uncharacteristic toughness.

"Fred! How can you even think of turning down this more prestigious position, and not only that...but one that doubles your current salary!"

I was momentarily speechless, but finally gathered my wits, and came up with my (for me) indignant response:

"I have two answers for you. The first is that Columbia Presbyterian has been my second home for the past 25 years. It nurtured me well during my training, and constantly supported my development as a doctor and more importantly, as a surgeon. I believe I owe it everything in return, and to abandon it now, despite the attractive offer by Roosevelt Hospital, would be, by my lights, close to treasonable.

"Secondly, the joys I have found in medicine come from caring for my patients, and not from administration. And I'm certain the job at Roosevelt would be mainly administrative."

Father sat silent. Then, shockingly, began to cry. He reached across the table and took my hand. "How could I have forgotten so completely what drives you? I'm ashamed of myself. Of course you must do what is right for you. And if that means foregoing fame and fortune, so be it. After all, you're the doctor. You're also my son, you have my blessing, and I'm proud of you."

I may be exaggerating his words, but certainly not his love. There were tears all around.

One of my father's greatest decisions happened around this time, one that touched all his sons. It happened on a red-letter day in 1961. He announced that he had made plans to take the three of us on a 7-day salmon fishing trip. In Canada! Lithgow Osborne was in on the plot, and had already negotiated with a small Canadian salmon fishing club on the Bonaventure River in Quebec. And so the Herters, father and sons and Osbornes, became the first American citizens to invade those sacred waters. Father's offer included 15 foot bamboo rods and reels with myriads of salmon flies, not one of which did we refuse.

Our week on the Bonaventure was a dream. Despite his arthritis, emphysema, and assorted malaises, Father had as much fun as his charges. We all 'killed' salmon. (That's right, killed. Because you don't just catch a salmon.) We laughed a lot, and any serious talk about life and death or the state of the world just didn't happen. Perfect Martinis were an essential adjunct to the late days. As I remember, the only time voices were raised was when Pa (as I called him) berated Lithgow Osborne for an improper bridge bid. Dad's apologies were served along with breakfast the next morning.

The fabulous week was replicated for the next three July's. And the in-between times were easily filled with replays and joy. By 1964, alas, Dad was in bed for the most part and dependent on oxygen tanks and various medications. Nevertheless, he did get out on the Bonaventure River one last time, and it was an episode I shall never forget. On the final day of our trip, Father, whose own total fishing time couldn't have added up to three hours, was determined to make a 'kill'. (His score for the week was zero.)

I kept my canoe close to his during his allowed time on the water. I was watching his every move. By then he couldn't stand in the boat, and when a long cast was needed, his guide would do it for him. Suddenly, after such a cast there was a visible and audible 'Strike!' The line grew taut and smoked its way out of the reel at speed. In the distance an enormous salmon leapt from the water, shaking its head to rid itself of the hook. During the jumps that followed, the guide somehow got the rod back into my father's hands. For a violent 10 minutes the fight see-sawed back and forth, with Pa in charge. He was weakening, yet he never released the necessary tension on the line. But the battle was shifting, the 'kill' never materialized, and the magnificent salmon flashed away, to live and fight another day. Pa was tearful and bereft. It was a sad, sad ending. For my part, I knew this day would be my father's last on the Bonaventure River...and so it was.

We left the next day, heartbroken but suffused with love for this fine man, our formidable father, each of us forlorn, fearful, and tearful that we would never see him again. Father died in 1966, far too young, at 71 years. For my brother Miles and me, there has been no end to the Bonaventure and the bittersweet memories it always evokes of our Dad. And that's why, for the next half-century, (50 years with only 3 exceptions) we returned to the Bonaventure, and even today, in Miles's 81st and my 90th years, we still talk bravely of going back. Chris died two years ago; he was as close, perhaps closer, to Pa than Miles and I, but fishing was never Chris's passion. Our sister Del, now in her 85th year, still sorely misses Dad, most of all for the fun she always had of baiting him politically. And that's just like Del.

A question: Could Pa, with his many commitments to public service, find the time or inclination to maintain old friendships, or make new ones? The answer, in short, is 'No'. For the most part, his friends were the ones he shared with Mother, and she was the one doing the work of maintaining them.

There was one exception. While he was at Harvard, Father made seven close friends, who on graduation, agreed to meet together every year, with or without wives. Lithgow Osborne was one of them. The name CALK was the group's insignia, mysterious until you learn it stands for Chicken ala King, its sternly undeviating menu. Annual meetings were observed with a miraculous regularity. I remember well one such meeting. It was in our house on P Street in Washington. This time wives were included. During dinner a challenge was issued to the members. Each had to prowl the streets of Georgetown, and the prize went to the first one who could inveigle some female to come back to the house with him, without enticement of any kind. The unlikely winner was Watty Washburn, a short, dumpy, former Davis Cup tennis player, who showed up with his captive in exactly 27 minutes. Watty's name is enshrined in CALK lore. (The other, more prepossessing members straggled back, companionless, over the next two hours.)

Would that Pa were alive today. I love to think of having Christian Herter's talent and character at work in Washington in these troubled days. It would be reassuring to see his tall, erect person tackling, once more, a leadership role. And wouldn't his left-wing brand of Republicanism find widespread support in today's hyper-partisan times?

Wearing his size-12 boots to the end, my father's unstinting service to his country was full-hearted and selfless. It remains an inspiration, not just to his family, but to the countless Americans who still miss him and salute his lifelong efforts to make the world better for mankind.

Another side of Mother and Father, playing charades at Cheehacombahee

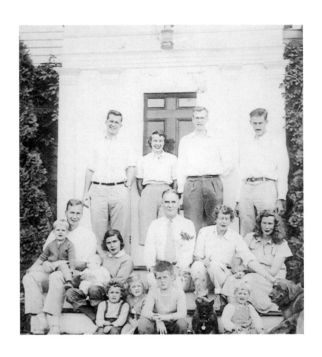

Mother and Father as Hamptonites

The Herter clan circa 1950,
in Mauchesta, Mass.,
post–Annabel

Mother, beautiful and loveable

Father, advising a young constiuent (his grandson)

Mother and Father, settling comfortably in Washington

CHAPTER FIVE

MOTHER, NUMBER ONE AT HOME AND ON THE CAMPAIGN TRAIL

(Sociable as Dad was shy. The Hostess with the Mostess.
A Disturbing Mid-life Romance.)

Mother was the same age as my father, and lived 14 more years after he died. From the preceding pages, which speak loudly of his political and foreign service, and, maybe more revealingly, of his attempt to reinforce his attachments to his children, one might think he was Number One in the family. Not by a long shot. It was mother who ran the roost. It was her that the children (and grandchildren) turned to with triumphs, problems, and family news. It was a certainty that Granny would always listen, and even better, always care.

We all adored her in equal measure for the boundless love she showered on us. She was simply fun to be with. She never went to college, had no intellectual pretensions of any kind, yet effortlessly made everyone around her, even the high and mighty, comfortable and joyful. It was her special gift. No one, but no one could throw a better dinner party, or be a better friend, or play a tougher game of charades, or love her dog, or cherish her children, than our beloved 'Mac' Herter. Moreover, I bet Father would be the first to say that she was the affable secret weapon behind his myriad public successes. She was an inexhaustible performer on the campaign trail, and she kept everyone's spirits up during the inevitable down times.

Looking back, it's easy to think of her skills in only the social sense. But she was an accomplished painter, and her favorite lifestyle was found on the family farm in Millis, Massachusetts. I can see her now, stately even wielding her trusty axe, whacking out a new trail, and opening a new vista. She enjoyed human companionship enormously, but I'm convinced that her long walks in the woods, with only her dog (and her thoughts) for company, were the rare and tranquil times she loved best.

Yet she was anything but a solitary woman. My, yes—she had admirers galore, and she never lacked a partner for the dance floor. But there was only one involvement of a serious nature. These days we'd probably deem it a midlife affair, though it seemingly went on forever. The situation was painful and puzzling to me, the more so because my father seemed utterly oblivious to its existence. As much as I was disturbed, my brother Chris, a junior in college, was blasé about the whole thing. Miles and Del were really too young to care... or even notice. My nagging concern about it undoubtedly sprang from my love for Mother. Perhaps I just didn't want any competition for her affections. On the other hand, my father's insouciance may have been based on some personal guilt from a dalliance of his own during Mother's near-fatal bout with typhoid fever just the year before.

Ah, well, we shall never know for sure. The mysterious affair slowed down while I was still in college, and ended soon afterward. It's soothing to think that the last two decades of my parent's lives appeared to be gloriously happy. It's a thought marred by only one exception, a youthful miscue on my part.

For some incalculable reason, I was driven to ask Mother to fill in the blanks before she died...to explain to me why she ever entered such a relationship... what role Father's aloofness played in its inception, and then why his acceptance of it had seemed so unfeeling on his part. With all these questions in mind I headed off to Washington to confront my mother with them. I never got the answers I sought. Instead, I'm afraid, I only induced a tearful sadness in her. Not for the act itself, I realized, but for having hurt me in process. Splendid mother that she was, she was never aware that her behavior could ever create unhappiness to anyone except her husband, but certainly not to one of her children.

And now, two generations later, the whole story remains untold. I regret, almost daily, that I ever asked the questions to begin with. It was an egregious mistake I can't forget, and pray I'll never repeat.

Mother (on the right) waiting her turn

Father is plucked from Cheehacombahee to become Ike's Secretary of State

Ike makes Father Secretary of State; Mother approves

August 25, 1917: Wedding bells for Mother and Father in Glen Cove

Forty years later in Millis

48

Playful days for Mother in Maine

Chris and Fred keeping watchful eyes on Father

Fred and Mother

Mother's seventy-fifth with her four children

Freshman at Harvard

Fred's passion: Rowing

Harvard JV, Number 5

Freshmen crew at Harvand, unbeaten. Fred at Number 3

CHAPTER SIX

AN EAGER BEAVER GOES TO LITTLE BEAVER, THEN TO DEXTER, ST. PAUL'S AND HARVARD

(Brother Chris, tormentor, protector, life-long friend. Glorious Grandparents, Gammy and Gampy. A Biking Blitzkrieg through Nazi Germany, Featuring Der Fuhrer and Smith Girls.)

Now let's go back to the Boston of 83 years ago, for my introduction to education. I successfully struggled through the travails of kindergarten at Little Beaver, learning to play the triangle in the band, and reveling in my brother Chris's gift to his classmates of crisp new $10 bills stolen from my mother's handbag! My family, however, thought that Dexter School, on the periphery of Boston, was the place I should next go to. It had style, reputation, was for boys only, and that is where I marched forth to attend first grade. But my second grade was aborted because of illness. Maybe I got sick of school. Anyway, I missed a lot of school and my family realized that if I were to get back to Dexter School, I'd have to somehow skip second grade. So they hired a tutor to give me an academic leg up.

My tutor was the great William Barry Wood of Milton, Mass, who became an All-Star at Harvard. He joined us at the end of his freshman year. In that year he'd been on all the sports teams and was an A student. In his next three years he won ten varsity letters; in football, hockey, baseball, and, finally, tennis. He captained his varsity team in two sports. At the same time he was not only Phi Beta Kappa but he was elected First Marshall of his class.

Barry Wood spent two months with us that freshman summer. The family had rented a house in Manchester, on the north shore of Massachusetts. I can remember him getting up at 6:00 in the morning, going out on the lawn and kicking footballs around. He was capable, pleasant, ingratiating, but utterly and absolutely humorless. Somebody had convinced him that to get energy from food you had to masticate each mouthful 60 times before swallowing. You can imagine how this went over with my family. By the time we finished dessert, Barry was still munching through his salad. It was off-putting to us, but he couldn't have cared less. Even as he sharpened my tennis game, he somehow put me through the second grade curriculum. And lo and behold, the following year I leapt, unencumbered, into the third grade of the Dexter School.

Barry went straight from his triumphant college career to Harvard Medical School, and, without breaking a sweat, moved on as a promising faculty member at Washington University Medical School in St. Louis. There he became the youngest full professor of medicine in American history. He ended his career at Johns Hopkins as Vice-President and Dean of the School of Medicine. By then, I was a doctor, too, and ran into him at various medical affairs. We'd have a drink, since he had graduated to martinis, and had even developed a sense of humor. So his company was a lot cheerier than when he was my 19-year-old tutor, and his endless chewing was greatly simplified. He married early to his childhood sweetheart from – where else? Milton, Massachusetts of course! And, naturally, the pair had three beautiful and bright children. Barry's only failure was in longevity. His brilliant mind was mismatched to a failing heart. Barry Wood was a man without parallel, and he lives forever in my mind for the 1941 Harvard Yale football game when he drop- kicked the winning field goal in the last minute of play! Barry Wood was nonpareil.

When I turned 13, after a decade at Dexter, I entered St. Paul's School., in Concord, New Hampshire. And I'm here to tell you that my five years there were among the happiest of my life. I loved every moment. Or almost every moment. Which is not to suggest that my life at home, up till I left, was not happy. Far from it. My younger siblings, Del and Miles, were in a different world, well apart from mine. But my older brother, Chris, was close enough in age to be my friend, although by god he was a vigorously competitive one. Where did this come from, his relentless competition with me? I was almost two years younger and certainly no match for him in schoolwork or sports and in developing countless friendships. Could it have begun one morning, several years earlier, when he threatened me in our bedroom with an ice-cold soaking washrag? (We slept in adjacent beds.) It was yet another way to establish his dominance. My smart aleck retort was, "You so much as touch me with that rag, and I'll throw your gold watch out the window!" I snatched his watch from the bed table between us, and held it up. A moment later I was sopping wet from the rag he'd thrown in my face. Just as quickly, I flicked his watch out the open window and heard the satisfying sound of its shattering on the concrete driveway, three floors below. He was wary of me from then on, and I'm happy to say that he now sports another watch that ticks along as faithfully as our friendship, neither of which has ever been in danger. It has, if anything, grown and grown with the passing years.

I had more than enough extra affection to truly love my mother and Mir, who was still part of the family. My affection for both mothers (real and surrogate) never left me, as I moved from home to boarding school. I still recall in particular one early Fall day, when playing touch football with my classmates. I crashed into one of the players, tearing beyond repair the sweater mother had knitted for me, and given to me as a birthday present. I dropped right out of the game, hiding my tears, afraid this would hurt my mother's feelings. Imagine recalling all that, after all those years! Those memories didn't include my father-- I simply didn't know him well enough in those days.

Another thought sticks to me after those first days at boarding school. Since I had played football every fall at Boston's Dexter School, I blithely assumed that St. Paul's would offer the same. Not for a moment! Football was considered too dangerous to our fragile, developing bodies. So they replaced it with Rugby! A game ten times more dangerous, because there was no protective padding. We wore cotton shorts and shirts, tackling our opponents while running full tilt on an open field. Moreover, the baffling rules for Rugby were impossible to master, especially for a 13-year-old New Englander. So when, in my first 'scrum' I grabbed control of the ball, I ran the wrong way, crossing the goal line of the opposing team. From me, tears, from my teammates, wails, and, I blush to this day, an over-response from my bowel department. But... had it not been for the kind arms of an unknown, older team-mate around my shoulder, and his warm, supporting words, I think my days at St. Paul's would have ended on the spot.

But the days went on, as days will do, I learned which goal line was which, my teammates cheered me on, and I survived, on the athletic field and even in the classroom. St. Paul's was a boy's school (girls came later, but perhaps better late than never.)

I was never the best at anything, academically or in sports. But I had my moments. When on the third football team of the Delphian Club (one of the three club teams at the school), I played end and had one of those miraculous days when everything went right. I tackled everyone in sight, caught passes, made blocks, gained yardage, and that night at dinner, the coach of the St. Paul's school team tapped my shoulder and said, "Unless I miss my guess, Herter, you'll be an All-American in five years!"

I was a fourth former then (a sophomore) and that game was my high point in football. I did make the first Delphian team by senior year, but not the school team. But who cares...my dreams of becoming All-American never left me. Anyway, rowing was my real love. St. Paul's had two rowing clubs, the Halcyons and the Shattucks. Each sported seven eight-oared shells and we rowed them on Long Pond, a beautiful body of water five miles from the school. We were transported to and from Long Pond on horse drawn barges, singing as we went. It was a magical, green and golden time. To top it all, my club, the Shattucks, fitted us out with the most elegant blue blazers imaginable!

The summers of my St. Paul's years had other charms. My older brother Chris and I spent two months with our artist grandfather, Albert Herter, in his East Hampton studio. We learned a little something about painting but never forgot our hormone- driven midday ocean swims with the nubile Brown sisters! Yes, romance of a sort. But the painting lessons were also absorbing. We started with a still life in sepia and ended up with the same still life in full color. These paintings still hang today in our kitchen upstate and, if I do say, I think they're remarkably good, considering our callow years, and the powerful distractions of those Brown girls.

Part of the summer's fun came from the young men helping Gampy, my grandfather, with his murals. Hart Ailes, I remember, and Gordon Grant, the descendent of the great naval painter of the same name. Gordon didn't give a hoot about the sea or the rigging of three-masters. His eye (and heart) was on the culture and dances of the Blackwood Indian Tribe of Montana, where he had lived for two years. And for ten dollars, I also became a member of that tribe, with my chieftain name of Otsquasochristseko. Try saying that, three times fast. Its American translation is easier: Blue Cloud. This naming occurred during a trip in 1931 to visit my Pratt grandmother in her hometown, Portland, Oregon.

Somehow, during the first of our Easthampton painting summers, I managed to edge out my older brother, Chris, this time by winning the affections of Gammy, our grandmother. She used to invite me to sit by her bed while she was served her tempting breakfast. For an hour or so, she would share with me her thoughts on her nighttime readings. A surprising number of them had to do with science or medicine...right down my later alley. Gammy, as it turned out, belonged to an intellectual salon in New York City, among whose members was Dr. Simon Flexner, the day's international expert on medical education and practice. I was flattered to be the audience for the intimate Gammy-talks, even if, truth be told, a lot of the content flew far above my puzzled head.

This is also a good time to tell you about Willy Stevens, my grandfather's principal model for his historic murals. How did they meet? Well, Willy was an orphan, without any known family but with a faithful Dalmatian dog and a job with the New York Electric Company. One day Gampy, an inveterate smoker, tossed his butt away as he sauntered down Fifth Avenue, caring not where it landed. Suddenly a man popped up from an open manhole, with smoke billowing forth from his bushy hair. Spotting my grandfather as the only prospective villain, Willy charged him. But under Gampy's easy charm, violence gave way to conversation and within minutes Willy had accepted the invitation to join my grandfather for cocktails at his apartment that evening!

This was the beginning of a beautiful friendship. Willy joined the group of assistants in Gampy's Easthampton studio, not as a painter, but as a model for the many U.S. heroes in Albert Herter's murals. And when Adele (Gammy) died in the mid-forties, Willy and his Dalmatian became Gampy's companions, and they drove across the country, visiting friends as they went. Much time was spent in Santa Barbara, California, the scene of Gampy's earlier El Mirasol days. Willie was a blessing---he remained faithful, friendly, and a guardian of my grandfather throughout those increasingly sad years preceding Gampy's death in 1950.

Here's an important fact, not about Gampy, but Gammy. A lot of people who knew them both thought she was easily his equal as a painter. Her portraits and flower paintings, small and few in number, were charming and beautifully presented. Her studio, a small space next to her bedroom was laughable in comparison to her husband's vast work place. Nevertheless, these two brush-wielders never failed to meet at 5PM to view the day's output at each site. They were each other's best (and kindest) critics.

Am I being indiscrete with this next anecdote? Oh hell, I'm going to relate it anyway. When Gammy was in her early 70's, she fell in love with a man half her age, named James Herd. What he did, where he came from, or what his apparent charms, I have no idea. Nor where or how he and Gammy met.. Young Herd was married to a dental assistant...that I do recall...and he appeared pleased to be the object of Gammy's affection. I met him several times on trips out to Easthampton. He was good-looking and well-spoken, but hardly on Gammy's educational or social level. On these family gatherings, it was painfully obvious that our tribe had a lot of trouble accepting the odd couple in their close relationship. Particularly my father. He hated Herd on sight, and once, in a rage, threatened to kill the man if he ever showed himself again on the Easthampton estate. I realize that doesn't even remotely sound like my father. I'm sure it was an attempt to protect his aging mother (and perhaps gain more of her love in Everit's absence.)

Grandfather (Gampy), meanwhile, showed a bewildering lack of concern at James Herd's constant presence in the house. To some, this raised questions about Gampy's sexual interests

Young Everit's wife (now deceased) was somehow convinced that Gampy was at least bi-sexual.

(If so, why should anybody care? He brought so much humor and love and beauty into this world.)

And now the long-ago plot thickens. One day, working as a Resident in Surgery at Presbyterian Hospital, I had a phone call from Harry Easer, my grandparent's genial jack-of-all-trades in Easthampton. He told me that a good-sized truck had pulled up to the front door of the house, and workers were now loading it with furniture. James Herd was officiating. When asked, he told Harry that Gammy had herself decided on this fabulous gift to him.

"What should I do?," Harry pleaded. I told him to get in his own car, and follow the truck wherever it went. Then call me. Frankly, I wasn't sure myself just what to do. When Harry called back, he said the truck had made stops at six different sites in Manhattan, leaving off furniture at each. I finally reached my father. His fury was uncontainable and his words unprintable. But his aforementioned threat to Herd was made publicly.

Neither the furniture nor James Herd was ever seen in Easthampton again. Gammy's adoration of this stealer of hearts and houseware melted away. Nothing more was heard or said

Until, several months later, a story appeared in the New York Times reporting how one James Herd and his companion, the wife of the president of the Metropolitan Life Insurance Company, had both drowned when their little skiff overturned in the waters off the South Carolina coast. My father's only comment: "I only hope that bastard's body doesn't wash upon the shores of Cheehacombahee!" (It didn't.)

But let's go back-to-school. I was anxious to see Europe, so in my fifth form (11th grade) at St. Paul's, I persuaded my mother to stake me to a cycling trip in Europe along with three friends from school. The agreed upon price was $250, which, if it can be believed, covered:

Two steerage trans-Atlantic boat trips. (New York to Bremerhaven; Cherborg to New York, and eight-to-a-cabin, all the way.)

The price of a heavy gearless bicycle in Bremerhaven.

A Retina camera in Munich.

Ten weeks of travel through Germany, Austria, France, and England.

210 marvelous meals, always including foaming steins of local beer.

As a topper (this was 1937), we had the thrill of hearing Der Fuhrer, Adolph Hitler, give one of his remarkable rants in the German town of Regensburg. None of us spoke the language but it mattered little – Hitler's body language during his Teutonic raving was surprisingly eloquent and understandable. One of my friend's fathers was so scared we'd develop Nazi leanings that he hired an English-speaking German graduate student to be our chaperone for a week or two. It was a poor move. This wild-eyed 22-year-old Hitler-Youth considered Der Fuhrer a deity, and our campfire arguments about Nazi politics often ended in tears, his tears. We were not sold, at least not for more than a minute, on Hitler's rejuvenation of Germany, nor were we surprised two years later by the onset of the war that was to encompass the globe.

As we pedaled southward through Germany on our monstrous backpack-laden bikes, our trip took a delightful turn when we overtook a busload of Smith College girls. From then on, we began each day a couple of hours ahead of the Smith bus; taking dangerous detours, so we'd arrive at the next town well in advance. There we'd be, seated casually in the village square, coolly quaffing our beer, as their bus pulled in, late in the day. Just think what unfettered testosterone can accomplish! Only Der Fuhrer, at his fiery best, was able to divert our attention from Smith!

It was a wonderfully illuminating trip and when my mother met us on return she was appalled by my brown teeth (cigarettes) but, in contrast, pleased when I reached in my pocket and pulled out $37.50 to give her, the remains of her original grub-stake!

I mentioned my academic mediocrity at St. Paul's School. That was modesty at best. But believe it or not, I did stay in the upper third of my class of 96 students, and for one miraculous marking period I ranked third in the entire school of 500. I was also a member of two academic organizations, one in science, the other in literature and debating. I even became a lowly editor of The Horae Scholasticae, the school magazine, and somehow won a medal for Best Essay of the year (on Thomas Hart Benton). But all that was hardly stardom. More important to me than such prizes was making friends, and I was lucky to forge such bonds of imperishable friendship with many of my classmates at St. Paul's. Infinitely deeper and more long-lasting than those from Harvard College or Medical School. These three aging teenagers joined me at our St. Paul's 70th Anniversary this last Spring! There we were, standing tall: Richard B. McAdoo, Haliburton Fales and Paul Pennoyer, and me. Paul barely made it to the reunion, and left us the following year. Maybe not the only remnants of our class of 1938, but at least the only ones well enough to show up. (At last count, November of 2009, there were but 7 survivors of our original 96 classmates, stalwart and true.) We three haltingly, but proudly, led the traditional school parade at what will almost certainly be our last anniversary. It was exciting and unforgettable, and yes, damn it all, moving.

Dick McAdoo was a publisher and writer (editor at Houghton Mifflin) and in these more recent days, a sculptor of note in Boston. Hal Fales was senior partner for many years at White & Case law firm in New York and, not incidentally, was elected president of the Century Association six years ago. Paul Pennoyer, of the Morgan tribe, was also a lawyer, specializing in naval issues. A pretty distinguished group.

Nowadays, as a matter of course, most boarding schools have both boys and girls in their enrollment. I often wonder whether single sex education is not to be preferred. Is anything to be gained by introducing that inevitable factor of distraction to the classroom or dormitory? I mean, how distracting can it be for teen-age males to be in class with the beings they were obsessed with 24 hours a day, anyway? My sister-in-law, Lee Herter, who graduated from a girl's school in Boston, has studied this at length over the years and is totally convinced that girls, at least, are better educated when sequestered within their own sex. It's hard to debate this point. But is the same true of boys? Possibly so. But the question of homosexuality always arises, as it did with us at St. Paul's in the early years. But there was innocence in our shared sexual awakening; it was a transient phenomenon and I never thought of it as misconduct, much less sin. Not so our rector, who appeared to me to have little understanding of adolescents and their sexual proclivities. In my sixth form year, my last year at St. Paul's, he called me into his office on my birthday, tossed me an apple, and when I caught it, said, "Frederic, at long last, I consider you a credit to the school." Oh, was I proud of this last minute approbation.

The 70th reunion at SPS. Hal Fales, Dick McAdoo and Fred

The glamorous grandmother, Gammy

Gampy's first love, painted 1891, originally valued at $900,000!

Great-grandmother Herter's block long masterpiece in Santa Barbara, CA (El Mirasol)

Gampy's famous mural at the Gare de l'Est in Paris, of the troops leaving for WWI

60

The Horae Scholasticae at Saint Paul's; I'm tall but in the back

Fred and son, Eric, also at Saint Paul's

Junior varsity with F.P.H. (circled) clowning as 'Beefcake'

Albert Herter's mural of French troops leaving for the front in WWI, commisioned by the French government and displayed in 1926. Everit, Fred's father's brother is circled in the window of the train on the far right. He was K.I.A. on the last day of World War I. The artist is seen on the right, holding the hand of Everit's son and facing Everit's wife.

ALBERT HERTER

1914 ·

EVERIT · ALBERT · HERTER · TOMBÉ · AU · CHAMP · D'HONNEUR · LE · 13 · JUIN · 1918 ·

63

At 12, I was dubbed Chief Otsquasokaseko (of the Blackwood Tribe, in Montana). Fred is circled.

CHAPTER SEVEN

MY EARLY LOVES

(My First Date, Age 11. A Near Date with Death in the Dakota Badlands on July 4, 1938, and memorable dates with attractive dudes at the Wyoming Ranch in the Month to Follow.)

I can understand how the reader might question my interest (or lack of interest) in girls.

I already mentioned the Browns of Easthampton, but my avid heterosexuality showed itself far earlier. My very first date was made, courageously, by phone, in my 11th or 12th year. (I can't remember her Boston telephone number, but it was close to mine, 5428.) The girl was an impossibly gorgeous blonde named Jean Saltonstall, of the famous Senator Leveret Saltonstall's family. The date-site was the Somerset Dancing School, on Boston's Commonwealth Avenue. The time was Friday afternoon, a week before the last dance class, and the annual supper event that followed. I really needn't have been so worried, because when I cemented my oral invitation with a personal call that evening, her answer was a definitive "Yes! I would love to!" Leaving me close to heaven.

Do I recall anything of that oh-so-special supper? No.

Or the days or the months following? No.

Because, after all, I was off to boarding school, with other things to occupy me, and Jean, understandably, cast her lovely eyes elsewhere. The elsewhere (somewhat later on) was Ben Bradlee, an old friend war hero, and legendary editor of the Washington Post, who brought down President Nixon, and, since birth, a friend of Jean's. That celebrated union was short-lived. Jean left Washington for Boston, and finally married my close friend and Harvard classmate, Bill Hausserman. Jean still lives, but alone now, and in frail health.

My second conquest (when I was 14) was even briefer that my first. While visiting my mother in Florida during her recuperation from typhoid fever, I sighted a smashing-looking girl who had just sailed into Hobe Sound. Smitten, and suffused with youthful ardor, I right off the bat invited her to the Winter Dance at St. Paul's. Just as quickly, she said 'Yes'.

And yes, she did show up at Concord, New Hampshire on time, and yes, I did recognize her (but just barely) but no, from then on she had so many friends that I was quickly forgotten. We danced only one dance, didn't even hold hands. Someone else put her on a train to somewhere, and can you believe that now, a short seventy-four years later, I can't remember her name.

Not a success.

But I did hold hands with, and even kissed, repeatedly, my next intended, Harriet Bundy, (fourth of the notable Boston Bundy tribe, sister of McGeorge Bundy, and Bill Bundy of the Kennedy Camelot years, plus their brilliant youngest sister, Laurie Auchincloss.) But nice as Harriet was, her formidable family was a bit high-powered for me, or, more likely, Harriet found me somewhat less than interesting. Either way, our attachment ended...but not our friendship.

The summer before college, I spent working at the Pass Creek ranch in Wyoming, along with my schoolmates, Joe Reed, Dick McAdoo, and I provided the transportation, a Chevrolet my parents gave me on graduation. Its top speed was 75 mph. In our efforts to outpace the police, we changed drivers every hour and we arrived intact at the ranch on July 6, 1938. Why is that particular date significant? Simply because two days earlier, on July 4th, we were passing through the Badlands of South Dakota, laden with lots of Roman Candles, scouting out the best place to set them off. The answer was not long in coming:

The absolutely ideal place for Roman Candles was the peak of one of the nearby Badland Mountains. Its height was barely a challenge. We easily scaled it, bearing our volatile fireworks. But the footage was a little scary, we slipped on the shale a lot, and our one flashlight soon flickered out. But we were young and foolish, and bolstered by beer. So our cry was 'On and UP!', till our gallant troop achieved the pinnacle, and never, NEVER, had such a Fourth of July Roman Candle eruption dazzled the eyes of South Dakotans. I'll bet they talk about it to this day. But also, as it turned out, never, NEVER, had the four of us come as close to ending our lives as on that foolhardy ascent. Because, in the light cast by our fireworks display, we saw, to our horror, that part of the upward path was actually a bridge of loose sandstone, barely a foot or so wide. Only McAdoo, our leader, made it across without disaster. He yelled at us to take a different path up, which we gratefully did. By the dawn's early light, we made the trip down, safely and joyously. Cravenly, we left the fateful bridge for more seasoned climbers to deal with.

The Wyoming ranch itself was beautiful, bordered by mountains to the Southwest, and about 20 miles west of Sheridan. The head honcho was Sandy Jacques, roughly as handsome as the Marlboro cigarette cowboy, and his wife, Jimmie, who was equally attractive. There was a group of other hands, in addition to us tenderfeet from the East. We performed routine ranch-jobs, and made occasional trips to the mountains to set up camps for the dudes. But the principle reason for our being there (to get back to the female theme) was to entertain and maybe even bring joy to the small but select covey of girls among the dudes. Not such an easy task, given our innocence, but we accepted the challenge, and the days (and nights) were not without happy moments. I can still remember a degree of competition between the four of us for the hand of a lusty and experienced 23-year-old who loved us all. Joe Reed and I, courteous and naive as could be, also fell madly in love with Jimmie Jacques, our hostess. We presented her with a bracelet or necklace, or some such bauble, as a symbol of our undying affection.

Shall I say more? I think not. But it was a glorious and maturing summer.

Then I moved on to one last pre-Annabel love. This happened during my second college year, and brought me back in touch with my Pratt family in New York. Sheila Crimmins (could there be a more attractive name?) was my cousin Caroline Pratt's best friend. They both went to Chapin School in New York and spent many summers in Maine or Connecticut. During one of their northwards visit I met Sheila, and promptly became her slave. She was tall and willowy, with dark lustrous hair, filled with humor and intelligence, a dream to talk to, and I fell for her on sight. Easily overcoming geographic differences, we managed to exchange visits between Boston and New York. Our last encounter found us at her apartment on Manhattan's Upper East Side. She had been to a Yale football game, and I was told to await her return from New Haven. Everything transpired without a hitch. Sheila returned, still glowing over a Yale victory, eager for a drink, but even more for a bath before going out for dinner.

So while I whipped up the drinks, she bathed, insisting that I do the same (in an adjacent bath). Soon enough we were side-by-side on a sofa, chatting away, but with no physical contact. I was puzzled, because our meetings in Boston were quite different. So I reached over to put my arm around her when, out of the blue, the window curtains parted and a man rushed toward us, laughing maniacally. Sheila, far from being startled, was also giggling away.

Who was this madman? Why all the laughing? Why was my confusion mixed with a sense of abandonment? It turned out to be a weird and mean-spirited joke. The laughing man was a Yale lineman, and a friend(?) of Sheila's. She had given him a ride to New York and brought him home, knowing that I'd be there, faithfully waiting. That's why she'd urged me to take a shower, giving him time to hide himself. I wouldn't have minded the awkwardness if I hadn't been so in love with Sheila. So instead of taking it all in stride, I acted like the callow youth I was. I poutingly packed my bag and stalked out, never to return or resume my courtship. Was I wrong? No doubt. But I was young and foolish and vulnerable. Isn't that excuse enough?

St. Paul's was, and remains, a great school despite (or maybe because of) its present female equivalence. I learned something of community living, of its obligations and responsibilities, and the meaning of noblesse oblige and our duties to society. I honestly believe that our time at St. Paul's left us better people and citizens. That's why I'm still angry that my grandsons felt differently. They went to other schools, to my mind not in the same class

Now here's another unbidden memory that welled up recently. At 13, when I entered St. Paul's I was burdened with an unpredictable voice which showed no sign of deepening. So it was no surprise that I found myself in the school choir's soprano section. There I stayed, happily in the treble scale, throughout the school year. Never for a moment thinking that my singing voice was anything out of the ordinary. So when I was named soprano-of-the-year at the graduation ceremonies, and presented with an inappropriate (but maybe prescient) gift of a silver ashtray, I was startled but pleased beyond words. In the succeeding years, as my body soared higher, my voice sank deeper; first to alto, and then to its final stop, baritone. Always under the guidance of the St. Paul's School choir. And I loved every note of it. As for smoking? It only started in my 17th year, when at last that silver ashtray award came into almost constant use.

Although music could hardly be called an essential component of my active later life, neither as a surgeon, or an academician in the Middle East, the chance to sing never failed to bring me joy. Opportunities to be tuneful were few and far between, but I never turned them down. As a matter of fact, my pal McAdoo and I managed a duet at our Harvard Club, and Boston dinner parties always expected vocal offerings from their guests. My brother Chris and I were called on to render "Dixieland' and "Wade in the Water", and that old favorite, "Who Stole the Lock From the Hen House Door?", all of them of South Carolina origin. I often added "The Owl and the Pussycat" and "Robinson Crusoe and Good Man Friday" to my repertoire. What fun it was and how we enjoyed ourselves, despite the gradual encroachments of age. But even these days, every once in a while, when popular demand takes over, I can be cajoled to pick up the mike, and, with my collaborators Gershwin, Porter, Kern and Berlin, attempt to show the young set how it should be done.

Back to my salad days. Whether you graduated from St. Paul's or many other New England boarding schools, you almost automatically got into whatever Ivy League college you applied to. In my privileged graduating class of 96 students, 36 of us went to Harvard, 30 chose Yale, and Princeton was not far behind. There was no problem whatsoever. But not today, oh no. Try as I might I couldn't get my grandson into Harvard, nor St. Paul's, for that matter. The playing field is much more level today than it was in 1938. And I believe that's a very good thing.

East Hampton's Brown Sisters

Manhattan's Sheila Crimmins

Fred horsing around at the beach

*A no-holds-barred bar in Sheridon,
Wyoming, after the rodeo, attracting
Emmet (upper circled), Fred and
McAdoo (lower circled together)*

Fred, already a lady killer, at almost eleven   Very early South Hampton woody with Fred aboard

Fred rowed No. 7 in the SPS crew, seen here second from the coxswain

CHAPTER EIGHT

FOLLOWING FAMILY FOOTPRINTS AT HARVARD

(Sex Education from an Innocent. A Raging Passion: Rowing!
My Impossible Dream: Harvard Medical School!)

1938, off to Harvard I strode. My father had gone there, my uncle had gone there, and my oldest brother was attending there still, a year ahead of me. And somehow it seemed appropriate that with my social and educational background, I should become a member of one of Harvard's clubs. And sure enough, I was tapped by the AD Club (Alpha Delta). Not as famous as the Porcellian, perhaps, but considerably more substantial (and sober) by those of us who got in. The AD became an important part of my college life, particularly its Lucullan breakfasts. My friend Dick McAdoo and I showed up regularly for the heaping platters of eggs, bacon, sausages and toast, but these were just an excuse for us to listen with awe to the night-before illicit adventures of an envied upper classman. This glamorous figure's impressive sexual conquests were described in lubricious detail, and since Dick and I were total innocents, we applied this erotic information to our burgeoning adventures of the flesh. A decade later at a New York dinner party, I encountered this ribald upper classman again, and gave thanks to him for my sexual education. He dissolved in helpless glee. "Oh, Fred, were you really that gullible? I made it all up, from beginning to end!" When I think of my wasted fantasies!

But back to Harvard: I just loved the place and I loved the people I worked with. If you asked what were my academic aspirations at that time, I would have to say none, zero. But my major was in fine arts and I spent the better part of two happy years in the Fogg Art Museum in Cambridge. It's a superb small museum, with marvelous teachers (among them Dr. Sachs). And as for fun? Oh god, I just loved it. Learning to paint in different styles was an eye-opening part of that fun. I didn't know what to do with it academically but who cared? I enjoyed every blissful moment. Not just art history, but the myriad mechanical details that go into creation. My thesis was on the iconoclastic architecture of Frank Lloyd Wright, a disturbing new star in the artistic firmament.

I was also a proud, if mediocre, skater on the freshman hockey team. I had been an average player at St. Paul's (but don't forget, 'average' at St. Paul translates to 'excellent' everywhere else). At Harvard that freshman winter, we lost 21 out of 24 games, and my skills on the ice were somewhat difficult to discern. The only cheers directed at me were when I took to the rink at Boston Garden, in our last game, and against Yale. I had just had my blades sharpened for this traditional set-to, and I couldn't control myself. I wobbled about like Frick & Frack, then crashed ignominiously to the ice. This can happen when your blades are too sharp. To the naive hockey audience (my mother and father among them) my ineptitude was regarded as deliberate clowning...hence the cheers. I was mortified, the more so because playing against me on the Yale team was Ben Toland, brother of Annabel, my bride-to-be. On top of all that, Yale, Harvard's arch –enemy, then as now, wiped the ice with us.

But the pain was fleeting, because I was already switching my athletic passion to rowing. That was harder than expected. At 6-foot-4in I was the smallest man on the crew! I was one of the few Harvard freshmen who had previous experience with this fantastic sport. So I not only made the freshman crew, but also was elected its Captain. We were unbeaten that year. In fact, we were so damned good, the varsity crew avoided us like poison. Especially after we left them in our dust (or our wake) when we first met on the Charles River. It was all unforgettably exciting.

The most memorable moment of my freshman year was our two-mile sprint back to the boathouse after we decimated Yale on the Thames River in New London. Our coxswain seized the moment, urging us on till we raised our efforts from 30 strokes per minute to almost fifty a minute. We were flying, borne aloft by our victory, and heedless of danger ahead. There was no way we could diminish this blissful and intoxicated finish. Except one. And that was when our gorgeously speeding shell, utter aquatic poetry in motion, smashed itself headlong into the pier, shattering into splinters, and dumping our gleeful crew into the waters of the Thames. What unalloyed joy!

Rowing, and my hearty oarsmen, kept me going back to the river my sophomore and junior years. And I made the Junior Varsity crew as a sophomore and in the next year, I jumped up to Varsity. Again, we had an extraordinary year.

But then, just a week before we headed for the Thames River in New London, for THE RACE (or Harvard Vs: Yale, as those others called it), we were preparing by doing racing starts against the JV crew on the Charles. During one heat, our coach Tom Bolles, a lovely man and good friend, called to have the boats come together. This boded disaster because it meant that changes were to be made between the two boats. I was rowing five, the middle of the varsity boat, and when he said, "Strokes change place," I thought, "Oh, thank god. Thank God!" I was a little saddened because the stroke of the varsity at that time was my close friend, Colton Wagner. But "Strokes change place", was followed by "...and fives!" and that's when my heart broke in half and died. What a catastrophic, what a dreadful finish to my idyllic existence on the Charles! Even more galling, I felt I was the better oarsman than my replacement. Oh, the humiliation!

This event abruptly ended my career as a varsity oarsman, but, as has happened a lot during my generally lucky life, this apparent setback actually set me on a different, and even more rewarding path, toward my years as a surgeon. There was no more downcast underclassman, and certainly not one who felt more sorry for himself than Yours Truly, as we jammed into the New York, New Haven & Harford club car down to New London for our Yale encounter. Despite my depression, I couldn't escape the infectious crowd spirit for "THE RACE". I can still summon up the unbearable excitement of that week at Red Top, Harvard's crew residence at New Haven, with Yale hunkered down at Gates Ferry. Then, fiercely partisan pleasure boats began to appear, each a larger and more luxurious yacht than the last, and burgeoning in number until the aquatic spectacle made us feel we were on stage. Even those without a mega-yacht to their name or the invitation to board one, could hoist themselves on board the special train that ran alongside the river, keeping pace, and cheering themselves hoarse, as they exhorted their struggling favorite.. The Thames teemed. The multitudes screamed. Ah, it was big, I tell you, it...was...BIG!

My melancholy continued to abate over each pre-race day, and I even came to admit, bitterly, that the varsity seemingly, just possibly, almost came within a hair of being better without me! The Thames River was wonderfully alive and a joy to watch and as THE RACE assumed its growing intensity, the attentions of the displaced Colten Wagner and I became almost exclusively directed to the coming three- mile Junior Varsity race.

The Day! Oh Happy Day! It was Harvard all the way!

The freshman crew skunked Yale in a two-mile race in the morning. For lunch, we knocked off the JV three miler by a half-length. For dessert, Colten and I watched with only slightly jaundiced eyes as the newly refurbished varsity crew won the evening race of four miles. And so, despite personal disappointment, despite unsolved plans for the future, it was a good...make that a great... day.

But as we rowed slowly back to the boathouse after our race, I felt quite certain that my rowing days were over, my heart was no longer in it, and my life was about to switch direction.

So there I sat alone in my room at Red Top, pondering my past and future and I remember thinking to myself:

"Jesus, Fred, you haven't done a lick of work for three years. Oh sure, you love the Fogg Art Museum and all it has given you, but is that really enough?."

Then I thought about my father and his entry into politics, and about my brother Chris in uniform, with the strong possibility of war ahead, and I felt very empty – and useless. Where should I go and what should I be to gain some purpose, some way to do some good in this fragile world, some way to give back those many things that I had been given?

In that doleful frame of mind, I grabbed a sheet of paper and a pencil and I warned myself, "Now think this through, Fred, think very carefully."

And at the top of the page I underlined: OPTIONS.

Under that I wrote, 'The Clergy' Hmmm. Now, granted St. Pauls's was a church school, but I'd become attracted less to the faith and more to the beauty of the chapel, its music and its silences. On the other hand, I'd been confirmed there. And in college I did work at the Christ Church, sort of, off and on. Certainly I puzzled over the popular pastor who ran the parish,, a wonderful priest, but a doomed man who committed suicide at the height of his career so I guess the church was still in my life, although I couldn't say prominently. A life in the ministry almost immediately lost it's place at the top of the list,

Crossed out, mercilessly. And to this day I can't remember what number two was. Maybe Curator or Art Writer? It may well have had something to do with the fine arts. But I erased that, too.. Number three on the list was, out of the blue, medicine. Medicine! This was a poser.

Because I swear that until that lonely night, I had never, ever thought about practicing medicine. Despite my famous great uncle, Doctor Herter, and those inspiring words of my grandmother in those early mornings at East Hampton. But, hang it all, the more I thought about medicine, the more the idea stuck in my mind. All of a sudden, it had many attractions. It was a dedication to the public good, which was important to me. And it suggested interesting problems that had to be faced and maybe even solved. It seemed to me that I was good with people and that that would be a valuable adjunct to a medical career. So, by God, by the dawn's early light, sweating out my future, I made it official: Medicine it was!

And early the following morning in New London, as soon as the lines opened, I phoned the Dean of the Harvard Medical School – who took my call. (As you can see, those were different days.) I took a deep breath and blurted out my rehearsed speech:

"DOCTOR-YOU-DON'T-KNOW-ME-AND-I-DON'T-KNOW-YOU-BUT-I-WANT-TO-GO-TO-HARVARD-MEDICAL-SCHOOL-THIS-FALL!"

"I see," he replied, "And just where have you been until now? and I said "I've been at Harvard!"

"I see, and can you supply me with your academic record from Harvard?"

"Yes!" I said, "Yes! Yes! But I have to tell you this right off the bat. I've really not worked hard enough, and I am at best a C+ man, up to now. But overnight, I've made what I think is a serious decision."

And this marvelous man said, "Well, you come in and talk to me if you wish, but I have to warn you, we're filled up for two, three, four years here, with brilliant young students, with splendid grades, who are just dying to get into the Harvard Medical School."

There wasn't a lot of encouragement there, but I went to see him when I got back to Boston and we had a really odd talk.

He said, "I've gotten your dossier from the college, and it's pretty miserable."

Then he added, "Now you're coming here and you're coming at a time when we're full up here, and we have really a very strong enrollment list for the future. To top that, you haven't even completed your pre-medical courses!"

Don't ask me how I got the nerve, but this is where things turned a tiny bit in my favor. Talking very, very fast, I said, "Yes, Doctor, I know, but I've done some research about finishing those premedical requisites. If I get myself to the University of Chicago this summer I can complete my organic chemistry and physics requirements. I've already completed, as part of Harvard's mandated agenda, one short shot at Chemistry One, all the basic stuff, you know."

He seemed a little taken aback by that, and said, "Well, I'm just so sorry and I hope everything works out."

Callow that I was, I thought he was impressed by my seriousness. At any rate, he shook my hand and he said ,maybe a little half-heartedly, "Goodbye, Fred. If things change, I'll let you know."

Thus encouraged, off I went to Chicago and spent a perfectly horrible summer. It was hot and miserable and I was in the laboratory for 12 hours every day, and I decided I really hated science, but I sweated it out and burnt the midnight oil, and against all odds, I passed both physics and organic chemistry. And when I triumphantly came back East, my family was still down on the shore in Manchester. I went there and smelled the salt air and told everybody I was glad to be back and I think I was glad I hadn't heard a thing from the medical school. But that silence didn't last long. The day after I started my senior year at Harvard, I got a blunt phone call. "This is the dean's office at the Harvard Medical School. We expect you to be in the anatomy laboratory at 9 o'clock sharp, tomorrow morning."

And to the many people surprised that I got into medical school with only three undergraduate years, let me say this: I agonized over that call all day long, thinking and rethinking my options. I finally looked in the mirror and told myself:

"Listen, Herter...here's a chance you maybe don't deserve and maybe you don't want to do it and maybe you do, but grab it, and prove with your lifework that Harvard didn't make a mistake."

Harvard's junior varsity edges Yale at two miles, in 10:06.8 to 10:10.6 in the day's closest race.

Winning THE RACE, by a nose, but only in junior varsity

Junior Varsity crew, Harvard sophmore year, Fred is fourth from the left

Fred as a young doctor, and even younger captain

CHAPTER NINE

MEDICAL SCHOOL IN ARMY GUISE

(Blending the Scalpel with Cloak-and-Dagger. Armed with a Pamphlet
"How To Deliver a Baby." And a New Doctor is Born. My Annabel,
My Son, My Move to New York.)

So I said yes and I was there at 9:00 the next morning. Sharp. The man who taught anatomy was a full four feet, eleven inches tall and hated me on sight. To him, I was a giant. But he put that aside and treated me just as nastily as possible. Anyway, I had made my decision albeit without joy and although the anatomy lab was frightening and smelly and I had no friends at my side, those things passed and I got to know my classmates, some of whom were suffering their own pangs of fear, or regret, or inadequacy. But little by little, the onerous work became more and more interesting, even fascinating, and before I knew it, the year passed.

I learned how to percuss the chest and probe the abdomen for liver and spleen, and even to unselfconsciously examine the breasts. I didn't end up at the top of my class; I wasn't that good. But I worked hard, ending up in the top third of my class at Harvard. Later on, though, when I took my specialty examinations here in New York State, I was told I was top man. That made me feel great. It had been such a long and difficult trial.

In getting into medical school when I did, I had no conception that World War ll was just around the corner. But that dread Sunday, December 7, 1941, Pearl Harbor burst upon us and we were at war. All the students in the medical school were immediately inducted into the military and we spent our remaining student days as Privates First Class. Our four-year agenda was reduced to three, just by cutting out all vacation time.

The Harvard Medical School and its students had little if anything to do with the on-going war, but some of the research going on in its laboratories was of potential importance. In particular, I remember the work done on blood preservation, and the mechanics of blood transfusion. I also recall the constant need for secrecy. One day, an army colonel on the administration team asked me if I'd serve as an information source. There were apparently some suspicious activities going on in the school. It was all very hush-hush. I was given a bogus name, and was instructed to report by phone, every Thursday afternoon, to a classified center in Cambridge. I can't remember my alias any longer... (Wait! Wait! It just popped into my mind: Dalrymple!), nor do I recall reporting anything of interest. But I confess I really enjoyed my James Bond role.

Even before being accepted by the Harvard Medical School, I had made up my mind, irretrievably, on two issues. The first was that I wanted be a surgeon, as opposed to other forms of medical care. Why was I so certain? Partly, I'm convinced, because my childhood was filled with the joys (and skills) of model-building, and the realization that working with my hands, using them as tools was essential to any form of creation I might embark on. If I'd harbored any doubts, they were all eliminated in the second year during the dog surgery course. This course was beautifully designed and as perfectly executed as any human procedures I encountered in later surgical training. The chosen dogs were treated precisely as a human patient would have been. The anesthesia, the antibiotic care, such as it was, the pre-and post-operative attention in the immaculate dog laboratory, and the skills taught and enforced during the surgery itself...all worked to fine-tune us as surgeons. The day-to-day care of the dogs, in and out of the operating room, made us more caring and considerate doctors. While it's true that when the dogs were operated on for teaching purposes, even when there was no medical need, an unpreventable degree of suffering was induced. But looking back, I think the natural affinity between humans and dogs made us feel their pain, and take whatever steps we could to alleviate it. I'm equally certain that the painstaking care and increasing hand-skills we developed operating on dogs, helped us save human lives later on.

And now, just for a moment , think of present-day surgical training. Should such dog-operations be allowed? Especially now, when other methods, such as lifelike robots are available? Obviously not. And yet...and yet...I sometimes think that the robots, however intricate, will never present the inevitable emergencies that arise during even routine operations, spurring a budding young surgeon to think fast, think on his feet, think of something unheard of, something daring, that just might save the day, and the patient.

But I can assure you, gentle reader, that this surgeon, at least, cared for those animals with the same loving attention we extended later on to our human surgical patients. And I am not alone in this.

When did I, for the very first time, find myself acting like an 'honest-to-God' doctor. And even believing it? It didn't happen until my second or third year of medical school. I was nervously on-duty in the Boston Lying In Hospital, dreading a call for help from some pregnant lady in our district who was on the verge of delivery. My role? Obstetrician, of course. And my unimpeachable credentials? Why, I had watched a delivery, twice, in the Hospital. So when the call came through, summoning Dr. Herter to help some woman in West Roxbury with her delivery, I was The Man!

Toting my doctor's bag filled with unfamiliar equipment appropriate to my function, I looked every inch a doctor, my authority diminished only by a pale blue pamphlet I was clutching, entitled: HOW TO DELIVER A BABY. I found that drive to Roxbury alarmingly short, partly because at every red light, I braked and tried to absorb the instructions contained in that magical pamphlet. It was an impossible task, of course, given that the traffic lights changed to green every 20 seconds, only adding to my serious qualms about my chosen profession. But my doubts were short-lived. When I finally found the house, and rang the bell, the door was opened by an attractive middle-aged lady who ushered me in, took my coat and bag and was utterly charming.

Moreover, after she denied having serious cramps, she asked me to join her at table for the dinner she had prepared for herself and her children. Relieved (and hungry) I did just that, and our conversation covered everything… everything, that is, except her advanced state of pregnancy. Finally, during dessert, the doctor in me took over, and, remembering the blue pamphlet, I suggested that I should carry out an examination. So we repaired to her bedroom, where I discovered that her 'cervix was not dilated'. Meaning that birth was not imminent. So, remembering the scant advice from the pamphlet, I suggested that the birth might be hastened by administering an enema. Which I did. And on my way to the bathroom to tidy up, I heard a scream behind me. Turning back, I saw my patient standing in the corridor , with the baby's head fully emerged! I yelled, "Run to your bedroom!" She did. I raced after her. And right then and there, and on the bed, baby and enema arrived simultaneously. Not the most sublime of sights, but my lady and her newborn seemed pleased, and together we took care of the umbilical cord and the messy bedclothes. When I left, some time later, everyone appeared happy, the lady with her newborn child, and her equally newborn 'Doctor', and my lifelong friendship with the family was secured. (Had the child been a male, he would have been named after Gary Cooper's son. Instead, she took the name of Gary's daughter.) Cheers! And shame on me for not remembering the name of such an unforgettable addition to my life.

My other decision was that after finishing medical school, I would leave Boston. Why? Well, the first reason was my father. Christian Herter was becoming well known on the political scene. He had been speaker of the Massachusetts House of Representatives for three years. Then the people sent him to Washington for the first of five terms as a congressman. Much as I admired and loved my old man, I thought it best we avoided impacting on each other. Selfish? Perhaps. In fact, when I think about it my reasoning seems a bit spurious, I suspect that I just wanted to make my way on my own without the boost that his successes in politics might provide me.

My other reason is that I was sick of being told each day in medical school that the only place in the world where proper education for medicine took place was in Boston. There was an arrogance, a chauvinism, which just rubbed me the wrong way. I was quite certain that if I went to New York City, I would find an equal level of medical education available. So one day at the end of the second year I joined two friends and took a trip to Manhattan. In one eye-opening day, we visited New York Hospital, Roosevelt Hospital, and finally the Presbyterian Hospital at Columbia. Of course it was impossible to gauge the quality of the surgical staff in such a short time, but we were favorably taken by the people we met. By the end of the day Bill Larson (from California) was accepted for future training at New York Hospital and Fred Jaretzki and I were accepted at both Roosevelt and Presbyterian hospitals. Was our mission accomplished? No, not that fast, that was all to come later. But we were mightily impressed and excited by the results of our adventure. Bill Larson did go back to California after his training, and Fred Jaretzki, after a decade of training in pulmonary surgery at the Mary Imogene Bassett Hospital in

Cooperstown, New York, returned to Presbyterian as my colleague. He built a brilliant career as a chest surgeon. Although Jaretzki and I favored Roosevelt Hospital initially, we found without much delay that Presbyterian was not only older but the more revered member of the Columbia family. That's where we ended up. And we never regretted our choice.

Never, not for a minute, was I disappointed for coming to New York. I had married Annabel Toland during my third year of medical school and we had a child, a son, Frederic P. Herter, Jr. (Eric), born in November of 1943. By September of the next year, the three of us bade farewell to Boston and ventured southwards to the place of my birth, and to my chosen New York hospital for training, Columbia-Presbyterian. I had had a long friendship with Annabel's family. Her father was head of the history department at St. Paul's and the Toland house was a short three miles from the school. Her older brother, Ben, was my close friend and a classmate. Ben was an unassuming Big Man On Campus, an effortless athlete and scholar, and the same outstanding qualities marked his college days at Yale. Ben's death on the beach at Iwo Jima was given wide publicity because of the way this splendid young Marine wrote his will. He had left his meager assets, half to organized labor, the other half to business. Somehow Time Magazine had picked this up, and lauded him, not only for his unusual bequest, but also for his valor and sacrifice.

Despite Annabel's being away at St. Timothy's School in Baltimore during much of my time at St. Paul's, we somehow managed to find odd times to join hands. Then, thanks to my sly persuasion, she moved from Vassar College up to Radcliff in Cambridge to give us further time together. You can't imagine how lovely-looking Annabel was, so full of life and joy, and our shared future together seemed inevitable. And so it was. Our pre-ordained marriage was celebrated at the Toland house in Concord, in May, 1942. It was a happy affair, replete with a goodly number of ushers and bridesmaids. All four of my grandparents showed up. Annabel and I were mere sprouts in contrast; she a blushing 19, I a mini-matured 21.

When we arrived in New York we rented an apartment just up the street from Presbyterian Hospital at 72 Haven Avenue. It was ideal, and comfortable, and had magnificent views down the Hudson. It was well worth the $75 a month rent. The only negative was the presence of cockroaches. I would like to say that over time they became my friends, but this was not so. My daily duty, after coming home from the hospital, was to rid the bathroom of these wretched creatures. But the rest of us were very happy there.

At the Presbyterian Hospital there were 12 interns in the department of Surgery and almost all of them became close friends. It was a joyful year for me, despite the ongoing war, the death of Ben Toland on Iwo Jima , and the fact that my brother Chris was on active duty in Europe. The attending surgical staff, my superb teachers, was clearly preoccupied, not with their remuneration, but with the love of what they taught. This led to an extraordinary closeness between pupil and teacher. At that time, and particularly after I returned from my stint in the army I felt that the Columbia -Presbyterian Hospital was truly my second home. I loved it. Still do.

I stayed at Columbia until I reached the traditional retirement age of 65. Despite the fact that I was fully competent in the operating room and had a busy practice and was involved in some on-going research , it was actually a good time to leave. I realized that in the middle 80's surgery had changed drastically in nature. It felt like I spent too much of my time at my desk trying to make sense out of the insurance forms of the government, of the state, or the community. Reams of paper work left little time for taking care of patients. The cliché "You've left at a perfect time" I heard a thousand times after retirement. I understood its meaning, on the surface, and spoken and unspoken. Regardless, all the while I was there I felt Presbyterian Hospital was the perfect place to be...and I was happy.

At last a doctor, Fred was able to make a bride of Annabel (1942)

Annabel catches a 3lb bass

Fred's catch, Annabel

Sleigh bells ring, in Millis, Mass, Annabel holds the reigns

88

Annabel's mother meets my grandfathers, Frederic Pratt and Albert Herter

Annabel and me, with Eric

CHAPTER TEN

A GREEN INTERN'S BAPTISM BY BLOOD

(A Dark-Ages Blood Transfusion. Oldfather Whipple, A Great Surgeon Bearing Tremors. Obstacle Course for Doctors, Under Live Ammo!)

Here are a few things I shall never forget.

The very first afternoon of my surgical internship at Presbyterian I was called and asked to go to the 11th floor of Harkness Pavilion where the rich and famous were housed, including an elderly lady needing a blood transfusion. This was something totally new to me. The apparatus involved in the transfusion did nothing to relieve my fears. The replacement blood was in an open-mouthed Erlenmeyer flask set on the top of a five-foot high wooden tripod, with nothing, but nothing to hold it there. And germs were prevented entry to this open mouthed flask only by an inverted Dixie cup. I stared at this primitive set-up and wondered why I had ever left Harvard!

But necessity is the mother of invention, after all, and soon, with the help of an experienced nurse and some adhesive tape, we secured the flask on the tripod. I busied myself searching for an appropriate vein in the patient's arm. I was crouched between the tripod and the patient, and to get a little more space, I pushed the tripod back with my foot. Alas, this pulled the tubing taut causing the blood-filled flask to tip towards me. Its contents hit the back of my head and then splattered over my patient. Blood, life-giving blood, cascading everywhere.

To make matters worse, which always happens, the door opened and in walked a visiting doctor from another hospital! He took in the scene and, God bless him, saved the day by roaring with laughter! Even that lovely blood-soaked victim in bed joined him in this hilarity and I finally allowed myself a grim chuckle or two. I retired to the bathroom, took off my ruined clothes, donned an open-back hospital Johnny and made my way down the corridor to the elevator bank.

I assumed that at best I'd be fired and sent back to Boston. But everyone's good nature prevailed and that evening I returned to the scene of the crime with my tattered dignity and sincere apologies. Thus began a long and lovely friendship with that grand lady. And, though I shouldn't take full credit for it, not only was a transfusion properly administered later by some senior doctor, but since that event, the entire procedure for blood transfusions at the hospital was changed forever. Not such an auspicious way for a young doctor to start his career, but I like to think it helped inoculate me against the arrogance that sometimes afflicts my kind.

Life seemed more civilized thereafter. My salary of $60 a month was slightly counterbalanced by the free meals we had in a special dining room replete with napkins and tablecloths and service. We could even invite our families on frequent occasions. And tradition had it that after lunch, many of the house staff would repair to the second floor house staff room where there were billiard tables and card tables and music. Serious competitions raged between the departments of medicine and surgery, and I recall one of our residents who swaggered about carrying his custom-made billiard cue in leather casing! But the time spent in such pleasures was limited. We worked hard, we were on call in the hospital every other night, and many were the nights in which we got not a wink of sleep. Such punishing hours are no longer legal and perhaps for good reason.

Another notable remembrance. Soon after I got to Presbyterian I was asked to assist in an operation to be done by the chairman of the surgical department, Dr. Allen Oldfather Whipple, a man respected and loved by his staff. As we scrubbed together , side by side, we began talking about our backgrounds. Whipple had been born in Aleppo, Syria. His father sold Bibles from horseback, covering about 25,000 miles throughout the Middle East. Eventually, our talk touched on the American University of Beirut in Lebanon, and Dr. Whipple's enthusiasm for "the finest educational institution in the Middle East" stayed with me. This innocent pre-operative chat became the basis of my involvement in AUB in years to come. Whipple was a superb surgeon. In fact, the procedure he invented for excising the pancreas for cancers was named after him. It certainly stimulated my later interest in surgery of that organ.

Here's a strange phenomenon. As his retirement approached, Dr. Whipple's hands began to tremble more and more as he began an operation. But contrary to the commonly seen "intention tremor" in which the trembling increases as the difficulty of the procedure grows, Dr. Whipple's tremor did the opposite. The trembling gradually ceased as the dangerous part of the operation approached. This unusual disability made each procedure with him an adventure, to say the least.

Because of the war, we were allowed only nine months of surgical internship before entering our mandatory two years in the army. So in the spring of '45, after the European War and my nine months as intern had ended, I left Presbyterian for the town of Carlisle in western Pennsylvania. Along with 300 other doctors, we underwent specialized military training. Because the Japanese had violated the Geneva Code by attacking clearly marked medical installations on the front, we doctors were taught not only to march in formation but also how to crawl under barbed wire, dodge 50 caliber bullets, and climb mountains wearing gas masks. The younger MDs approached such arduous activities as a lark, but two of the older doctors perished in the process. Annabel and I made a happy time of it. She learned how to fly single engine planes and during our outdoor lunches she would appear overhead and wag her wings at us. One day we staggered in from a forced 25-mile march. I never dreamed I'd be able to do such a thing and live, but I was young and bursting with health. Anyway, that day, up there on the bulletin board was a three by five card saying – and I can see it in my mind's eye, and I still shudder:

"Today a bomb equal in force to 20,000 tons of TNT was dropped on the Japanese city of Hiroshima." My mind reeled. But it took some time to realize just how hideous this act of war was. With the next atomic bomb (the only two nuclear weapons used in the war), on Nagasaki, the Japanese war ended, and the inhuman consequences became known, not only of Hiroshima and Nagasaki, but also from the heavy bombing of Tokyo and other major cities of Japan.

CHAPTER ELEVEN

HIROSHIMA BRINGS PEACE WITH JAPAN, BUT WORLD-WIDE ANXIETY

(A Sudden Peace for Others, not Me. Prisoners of War; the Hitler Youth. Annabel and the Hypnotist.)

It felt strange to me to be still in uniform, with the world suddenly at peace. But then I got my orders to report to a military medical center in Tacoma, Washington. The next thing I knew, I was cruising across the country by car with Clay Frick and his wife, Lo. (Annabel and our son Eric skipped this trip and opted to join her family in New Hampshire.)

At this general hospital, I was assigned a post in surgery, having blithely faked my experience in this specialty. Up to then, I had done exactly two appendectomies and a single hernia repair! That was my entire resume. But for a short while, there I was on the surgical service, operating every day. The only possible reason I got by was that I was operating on young men who were in very good condition and I was doing relatively simple operations. I did many hernia repairs and some appendectomies and one or two other procedures that apparently matched my level of expertise. I was also forced to assist some senior medical officers in performing simple operations. Many of my superiors were totally untrained in surgery, and I found myself instructing them in basics. Little things, like which side the hernia was on!

To me, the most absorbing aspect of my Tacoma interlude was the care of prisoners-of-war. They were sequestered in four wards of about 20 beds each, each ward assigned according to patient nationality. But the Japanese and Italian prisoners were treated a little differently. They were thrown in together, noisily and unhappily. Sickness was endlessly feigned by both groups to get attention. True sickness was somewhat rare. These, after all, were robust young soldiers, well-fed, and pretty well cared-for. I found the German POWs the most interesting. The first group, captured early in Africa, was the Hitler

Youth. They were bitter, aggressive, and disdainful of their captors, and they were sequestered to a ward of their own. The second group was made up of the oldest and youngest of the Germans who were taken at the European front toward the end of the War. So they were mostly free of Hitler's influence, and saddened by separation from home and family, and the loss of comrades-in-arms. All in all, these were a decent lot, friendly, grateful for our care, and still capable of laughter.

In fact, so different were these two German groups that we didn't dare to let them mingle during their outdoor exercise periods. One of the 'good' Germans was killed by the Hitler Youths during an earlier encounter.

The fourth ward under my control was American. These were prisoners, not of war, but of criminal acts while on active duty in the Army. I was happy to restrict my visits to serious medical attention.

A typical round on the German wards would go like this:

Otto, my interpreter, would stand at the entrance to the ward and wait until precisely 8am, then bellow..."ACHTUNG!"

The militant Hitler-trained youths would immediately spring to attention, regardless of their affliction, whether broken bones or recent surgery. Only on my command, also yelled by Otto, would they sit or lie down, so I could examine, or change a dressing. And nary a smile or a word or a thank you. Hardly an amusing exercise in encouraging bedside care.

Ah, but then! We approach the second German ward. What a difference. Otto's "ACHTUNG!" was followed by several "Guten Morgan's and a smile and a cooperative posture that made my examination simpler and more effective. I also sensed their joy in realizing that a doctor from the enemy fold could care about them.

Suddenly it was Armistice , the 11th hour of the 11th day of the 11th month of the year. The day was still widely celebrated. When my young German friends (and prisoners) asked me what all the fuss was about, I lacked the heart to tell them about their defeat in World War One. Instead I explained, "What? Didn't you know? Tomorrow's my Birthday!"

Fair enough, because November 12th is my birthday. Always has been.

I didn't give my fib another thought. Not until I began rounds the next day, November 12. Otto blurts out "ACHTUNG!" and there's a resounding chorus of "HAPPY BIRTHDAYS!" in speech and song. All who could muster the strength, stood proud beside their beds, bright-eyed and bushy-tailed. And the celebration never ceased that remarkable, memorable day.

Cakes and ice cream, more song, more cakes and ice cream and, I think... even a drop or two of wine. Apparently, not a prisoner on the ward slept a wink the night before...they were all happily at work in the kitchen!

It wasn't long after this affable celebration that the repatriation of my prisoners began. Formal farewells were forbidden, but why should that be? I certainly managed some tearful goodbyes to my German brothers under-the-skin. And back-and-forth letters between me and Otto, my faithful interpreter, continued over time. It was a strangely interesting and affective interval in my duty as an Army surgeon. I wouldn't trade a day of that period. Not for anything.

My Tacoma time lasted three or four months. Annabel and Eric joined me, and we rented a pleasant house on American Lake nearby. Days were happy at first, but though I initially denied the signs, towards the end of my assignment it was unmistakable that Annabel was growing more and more depressed. I was concerned, but not concerned enough to get her the appropriate care. I had minimal training in psychiatry at medical school and we were in unfamiliar territory, so I let myself believe that her condition was transient and not serious. But then we had dinner one night with a surgical colleague from Texas whom I never liked, but I felt we had to oblige. At dinner this doctor gabbled incessantly about the greatness of his home state and things he had done, and oh yes, how clever he was to make his surgical incisions so short!

Then, in the middle of dinner he said, "I happen to know how to hypnotize people. Would any of you like to be hypnotized?" I almost fell over when Annabel raised her hand. So after dinner he did, in fact, hypnotize her and put her through some physical stress tests that I wouldn't have believed possible. He made her hold her arm out sideways and then got others to swing on the outstretched arm. It was an extraordinary and impossible feat under normal circumstances. The hypnosis went on for a half hour, then he said, "Now I'm going to waken you and when I do, two things will happen. First, you're going to feel happier than you have in your entire life, and secondly, you're going to ask for a cigarette." (Annabel didn't smoke).

Well, it happened just as he predicted. Annabel wakened and was not only her old pre-depression self, she was a little bit more. Suddenly, out of the blue, she asked the man next to her, "Do you have a cigarette?"

It was certainly a remarkable performance, but something about it bothered me. As we were walking home that evening she said, "My God, Fred, I feel so much better!" And she appeared to be just that. But a couple of days later, this man, the Texan hypnotist, called her and said, "How are you feeling, Annabel?"

She told him, "It's amazing but I feel so much better."
"Well, I think we should meet again." And so they did, but without my knowledge.

Predictably, there was no repeat of hypnosis. Instead, he made repeated and clumsy passes at her, which ended, permanently, whatever personal or professional relationship may have been in the cards. Thank God. The man was a miserable creature, someone to be avoided like poison.

During the next weeks Annabel gradually moved up from depression, obvious depression, to normalcy once again. And by the time I got shipped off by boat to Japan to join the occupation army, she was in great shape and I convinced myself that her problem was transitory, a passing fancy and that to leave her was safe.

CHAPTER TWELVE

TO JAPAN BY SEA, TO JOIN POST-WAR OCCUPATION ARMY

(A Truly Sick Sickbay. Aiko, the Tender Maid who Bathed Me, and Seventh Day Adventists who saved the Day!)

And so I traveled to Japan, a 14-day trip across the Pacific along with 200 doctors, and an even larger group of non-commissioned officers. The small liner belonged to the so-called Presidential Line. I think it was called the General Hayes or something close to that. I even knew the tonnage at one time. But during that seagoing period I learned a little bit of Japanese, not much, such as 'Benjo wa, me doko arimaso?" Translation? "Where is the nearest toilet?"

We boarded ship in Walnut Creek, California, sailed down river to San Francisco Bay, then circled Alcatraz twice to correct our compass position, and steamed West under the Golden Gate Bridge, into the heavy, rolling, endless swells of the Pacific. By morning, most of us were in the unbearable throes of seasickness including myself. And, to make things even worse, I was given the enviable assignment of running the sickbay. Not a happy beginning.

In Yokohama, our landing port in Japan, I was assigned to take a group of soldiers, some 300 or 400, by train down to Kyushu, the southernmost of the Japanese islands. The trip took almost three days. We ran out of water; the troops on board had nothing but C-Rations (Spam). We ran short of those, too. So there I was, a young First Lieutenant, Medical Corps, with a near mutiny on my hands when the water source dried up. We had to stop the train and drain water from the boiler of the engine and drank it as it cooled. That made people less cantankerous. The boiler water lasted the rest of the journey, to everyone's joy. But all in all it was a miserable trip, particularly since it was on my watch.

We finally arrived in Kyushu, where I said goodbye to my charges. They were happy and so was I. I was sent to an officer's dwelling where I was asked to take off my shoes, the usual Japanese custom. I was promptly assigned to military government (public health) which meant I had very little to do with medicine, at least in the conventional sense. I was sent to a small city in Miyazaki-ken, a province of seven million people. And of all the strange things, somebody came out to see me almost immediately after my arrival and said (through an interpreter) "This is the happiest day here we can imagine. I understand that you are well known in your country for your work in public health, and we're having a meeting here of all the public health officials in Miyazaki-ken. There are 500 of us and you would do us the greatest honor of coming to speak to us this evening."

What a perfect place for a 24-year-old who knew zero about public health. What could I possibly speak to them about? I didn't know the difference between an anopheles mosquito and a chicken hawk. I knew nothing, nothing at all. But they gave me a translator, and I found myself in an auditorium facing this mass of professionals who knew everything. It was not my favorite night. The only thing that alleviated my misery was that after I said something, the translation had to be delivered and during that period I had enough time to think what I would say next. I got through it. I said nothing of substance, just how happy I was to be there and what a beautiful country you have and I'm sure that you're handling the public health situation with great ease and skill. It was awful. But they were so kind and courteous; they thought I was great, absolutely great, and when the convention ended a day later, I received an obscene number of presents, mostly in the form of dolls, beautiful Japanese dolls to take home to my family.

The convention's end left me still in charge, still not knowing anything. I lived in a place called Beppu on the northeast coast of Kyushu. An incredibly beautiful place: a lovely harbor with mountains surrounding it. Hot sulphur springs from them fed our baths. It was utterly untouched by war. I lived in a charming Japanese house with three other junior officers (lieutenants). It had a lovely garden surrounded by four bedrooms and each bedroom had an exit into the garden. My office was in Oita, the provincial capital, several miles from Beppu. The office was capacious and comfortable and the hall leading to it had a red runner symbolizing my importance. And I had a maid – oh, dear, isn't this awful, my memory is so bad – an absolutely lovely young girl who came from a good family. She spoke no English, I spoke no Japanese but somehow we communicated. Her name just popped up: it was Aiko. There was no hanky-panky whatsoever. When I would come home from work, I'd have my boots on. She would take my boots off and she would ask. "Beeru? Whiskey?" And she would reappear with an icy beer, and then we'd head off to my room and she would undress me, and I mean totally, and lead me by the hand down the hall to a bath. Yes, a tile bathroom, quite beautiful, with a bath itself about three times larger than our conventional tubs. She would wet me down, then soap me from top to bottom and then rinse off the soap and I would get into the bathtub to soak for perhaps 30 minutes – very, very hot. It was enervating but happily so. And after leaving the tub she would take me for a walk outside the house until I had cooled off. It was heaven, but come to think about it, no more than I deserved. Ha!

Then back to my room where she would dress me for dinner, meaning clean shirt and tie (no uniforms in military government) and I'd climb to an adjacent house above us where all the senior officers lived. They seemed pleased to see me (largely because I said 'Yes' to their invitation to play poker after dinner). I played too, but without much skill, didn't 'know when to hold 'em, know when to fold 'em', and by the end of the first week I was yen-less.

I stayed from then on with my unit and with Aiko in the junior house. We'd sit on a jute mattress and we sang to each other. I sang American songs, she sang Japanese songs, none of which I remember. No. One of which I still remember and embarrass my Japanese friends by singing it to them. But those days were simple and lovely and I think Aiko became to a degree enamored of me as I was of her. We never even held hands, but she was enchanting and she lent joy to my weeks in Beppu. The public health aspect, in contrast, couldn't have been more mundane and devoid of interest.

Our unit moved from Kyushu, that southernmost island, to one to the northeast, Shikoku. It was smaller, but lovely, even enchanting, and there I spent a priceless month. The time was blighted only by another medical officer whom I absolutely couldn't stand. He was a totally humorless man, he came from a humorless religious background and he played a humorless guitar and sang humorless hymns. I can't imagine why I disliked him so. As American occupiers, we were not allowed to go into Japanese homes. One day, my boss, who was a colonel, said there was doctor in the village who'd very much like to have me and my medical colleague for dinner. This was unusual – had we not been doctors it would have been totally disallowed.

So we went, full of curiosity and anticipation (it was our first night out on the town), and the family engaged us in a beautiful and mesmerizing tea ceremony. But the dinner was disappointing - U.S. Army issue SPAM- with which we were all too familiar, and to my even greater dismay, my religious colleague pulled out his guitar after dinner, and began his infernal strumming and started to sing a hymn. But to my wonder, from the back of the room, I heard this high soprano voice picking up the tune and singing, and then singing not American but Japanese verses. It turned out that they all, my colleague and this entire Japanese family, were Seventh Day Adventists. Despite that, or maybe because of it, it became an unexpectedly interesting evening.

CHAPTER THIRTEEN

A DEAR-JOHN LETTER ARRIVES.
(BY TELEGRAM)

(Annabel's Sickness and Tragic Death. I Discard the Uniform,
and Step into Scrubs.)

Then came sadness. I received a telegram (there were real telegrams in envelopes delivered in those days) from my wife saying that she had fallen in love with another man, a lawyer from Concord, New Hampshire. She had asked the Red Cross to get me an emergency leave so that I could come home and perhaps settle the issue with her. Never would I have foreseen this coming, even after Annabel's former depression – and I couldn't believe it. But the next day I found myself on a plane coming back to the U.S. with a group of fellow Dear Johns. These were army personnel returning home for the same reasons – marital problems at home. I was sick at heart, unsure of my next steps, and I must say I deliberately took my time getting there. When I arrived on the west coast I took a train from San Francisco to Boston. It took three days and I was hoping it would take much longer. I was just terrified.

When I finally arrived at Boston's station, Annabel was waiting. She looked quite unlike what I remembered of her when I left San Francisco for Japan. She was pale, nervous and as we self-consciously stood there, she pulled out a cigarette and started smoking it – a remembrance of the hypnosis evening. And we went from the train station to the middle of Commonwealth Avenue where there was a grass strip, with trees. We sat there and talked for over two hours, but I got nowhere with her. She said she'd been visiting a friend, Ruth DuPont, in the Adirondacks. Ruth told me later that while she was there Annabel was on an absolute high and she'd written an entire book in the seven days of her visit.. I didn't know what the book was about, I never got a copy of it. At any rate, she was now a different person and I said, "You sound different, you're behaving differently, you're not the wife I had when I left, and I'm not sure what's happened but you clearly need help, and I'll try to get it for you."

I'm not sure whether I said all that but I'd like to think I had, and perhaps I had. Clearly it was a situation calling for the wisdom and judgment of a professional therapist.. But I'm afraid I didn't convince her of this.

So we parted and I went to see my mother and father. Naturally, they were upset too. And I learned that Annabel had been wildly insulting to them. Not only excusing her own behavior, but accusing them of having had affairs themselves. True as that might have been sometime long in the past, it was ill received by both my mother and father. They were not happy about the situation. Not one bit more than I was.

Two weeks passed. I met with Annabel several times, trying to get her to change. She would have none of it and finally I faced her with what I considered to be the critical question: "I understand you still want a divorce, but what about our child?" And she said in so many words, that's entirely up to you. It was a shocking blow from someone who loved Eric, as much as I knew she did. Even then, after such a clear sign of her sickness, I balked at seeking out a psychiatrist. How could I have been so stupid? So insensitive? So unknowing?

Instead, I went to see a family solicitor named Harvey Bundy. He was a close friend to my family, a well thought of lawyer in Boston and incidentally, the father of all those famous Boston Bundys who figured so prominently in the Kennedy administration. I'd never been particularly taken by Mr. Bundy, but he couldn't have been nicer or kinder.

He said, after we had talked, "I think what you should do is give this time. It will probably blow over. If it doesn't, we can go through the motions but the one thing I must insist on is that you go through separation and divorce proceedings separately and you must stay in this country where the residency requirements are often of length. You can go to Reno, of course, and in half a day you can get a divorce. But my suggestion would be Florida where there is a six month's residency requirement before any kind of separation can be obtained.'

Bundy's suggestions seemed reasonable, but I further insisted that a nurse of my choosing should accompany Annabel and Eric in Florida. So I conducted a search and I found a marvelous woman, youngish, but old enough to be full of sense. She came, met Eric, and off the three of them went to Boca Grande,

Florida, where the Toland family had a small cottage.

During that ugly period I didn't hear a word about the Concord lawyer with whom Annabel had supposedly fallen in love. Not a single word, not a whisper.. And in July of 1946, when she left for the south with the nurse and our son, Annabel was still high as a kite and intransigent.

Meanwhile I had been sent on an interim medical assignment in Texas, and from there drove up to a small military hospital in Seattle, Washington. I stayed in touch with the Florida situation by phone but I particularly remember the 23rd of November because it was our son's third birthday. I remember also Thanksgiving Day in 1946. On this occasion I talked to both Annabel and Eric. To my ears, and for the first time in this long period of absence Annabel sounded less sure of herself. At the end of this talk I pleaded, desperately,

"Annabel, for god's sake, get on the next train with Eric and come out here. I want you and this is where you belong." She didn't answer, simply hung up

Two weeks later, on the 6th of December, 1946, I got a call from Annabel's father.

"Fred! Something terrible has happened. Annabel's had an accident! That gun she had in the Florida house went off by mistake, killing her"

Oh God, oh no, oh no. No! I couldn't, wouldn't believe it.. But Ned Toland went relentlessly on: "There were only women in the house and I thought she should have a gun just in case. So I gave her one, loaded it and put it in the closet of her bedroom. She discharged it by accident and that's the way she died, I'm sure of it."

And I thought immediately, this is not the way she died. She killed herself and I'm sure that is what did happen, despite the kind interpretations of her father.

And only this past year could my son Eric, then 3, now 66, fill in his account of what happened. I asked him, "Eric, do you remember anything?"

"Yes, Dad. I was right there in the next room but I heard the noise and the commotion and I knew she had died. I don't know why". That was the first time he had spoken of his mother's death in all those 60 years.

It was a dreadful time. It was sad beyond words. There was a service for Annabel in Philadelphia, which is where the Tolands came from. And the older brother Dale was there, but not Ben, who had been killed at Iwo Jima.

But a number of people came - family, friends of hers, and she was buried in a cemetery near Philadelphia. Poor, dear Annabel. She deserved more of life. And that was that. Except of course, that wasn't that. It never is. To this day I suffer the guilt of not having seen the early signs, and lacking the sense to seek professional help for her when it might have made a difference.

I must add further sad notes. Mrs. Toland, Annabel's mother, also tried to take her own life, but failed in her mission. And her older son, Dale, took the same route. After a successful period in St. Louis as Treasurer of the Monsanto Company, he lost his job, lost his wife, and was left with two children. Later he remarried, apparently happily, but then, suffering from who knows what, threw himself out his 14th floor room at the Yale Club in New York City. Leaving us with the quandary: "Can we ever fathom the utter loneliness and terror it takes to inflict such harm on ourselves, and those we leave behind? "

Two of Dale's children by his first wife survive; Edward D. (Neddie) followed in his grandfather's footsteps by heading the history department at a high school on Cape Cod. And Frannie, an artist whose marriage to Pulitzer Prize winner Tracy Kidder, has been supremely happy. Or so I've been told by my son Eric, who sees them periodically.

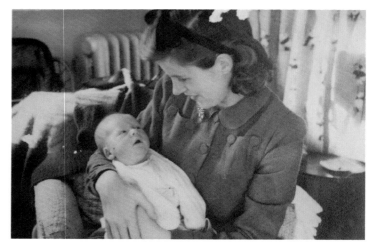

Eric's first date with a camera, and his mother

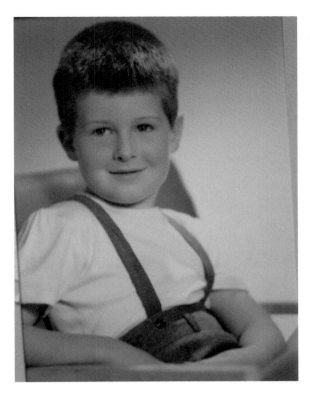

Eric at two, with an unknown companion

Eric at four, already camera-wise

My pride and joy, two girls and a boy. Brooke, Eric, and Caroline.

My fair lady!

CHAPTER FOURTEEN

...AND THERE STOOD...SOLANGE

(I Marry Dad's Congressional Secretary, Harriet. 29 Years Later, Lady Luck Smiles my Way, in the Form of Solange.)

After Annabel's funeral, I went back to fulfill my time in military service, and in February of 1947, I was discharged and back at Columbia again to finish my internship and move into a full residency in surgery. I was going through a rough patch. The hospital work was arduous, it was difficult to find time to see Eric, who was staying in Washington with my parents and attending school there. Of course, sorrowful thoughts about Annabel never really left my mind.

When Annabel died, my father was in his second of five terms in Congress. He was busy beyond belief and I'm sure the arrival of two-year-old Eric to the household was not greeted with total joy. But he and my mother and the nurse I had hired were more than supportive and Eric's entry into a local Washington school went smoothly.

I came to Washington as often as I could to spend time with Eric (and family). As fate would have it, in the spring of 1947, I became attracted to the young lady who ran my father's congressional office in D.C. Harriet Conel was bright and comely and had been well-educated at Smith. Her father was an academic anatomist at Boston University. I was sure that some of the letters I'd gotten from my father when I was in Japan, which were done on a typewriter, were of her making. Anyway she was an engaging woman.

As it usually does, one thing led to another, my trips to Washington became more centered on Harriet than on Eric, and at the end of November of 1947, we were married at St. Thomas' Church in New York. I realize now that my decision to marry, so soon after Annabel's disaster, was premature.

My reservations about our future were magnified when Eric came to join the family in New York. He and Harriet were at loggerheads much of the time. Harriet was jealous of Eric because he was mine and close to me, and his stepmother's misinterpretation of his apparent sexual aggression toward

107

her (Eric was three) were beyond her comprehension or approval. A child psychiatrist at Presbyterian did his best to improve their relationship but without avail. But separation or divorce in those days was out of the question, particularly in that traditional hospital of mine, and I lived through it all. Am I stressing the negatives? Yes. We tried to have children and in 1954 and 1956 succeeded. Two beautiful and lovable daughters, Caroline and Brooke, brought joy to the household, and with Eric off at boarding school, life became more serene. Harriet adored the girls, as did I, and my frequent absences to surgical meetings away from New York no longer carried the dread (to Harriet) of lonely nights at home. The greatest threat to our marriage was not Eric, as I hope I've suggested. As the years passed, the relationship between Eric and Harriet warmed to a degree...both were bright and intellectually curious, and their common interests led them to friendly exchanges. No, neither Eric nor Harriet was at fault, it was I because of my obsessive, all-consuming fascination with my work. Poor Harriet found little interest in medicine, my workdays were impossibly long, and her fear of flying meant she couldn't travel with me to distant sites for crucial surgical affairs. Our social life, in Dobbs Ferry or New York shrank to almost nothing. And for this I must take much of the blame.

Our summer vacation months in Maine were by far our happiest time as a family. The children loved Maine, I loved Maine, and for Harriet, since there wasn't any competition from my surgical life, she also loved Maine. Perhaps to a greater degree than the rest of us. That's maybe because her childhood summers were spent exclusively on Bailey Island, in her parent's seaside cottage.

We stayed together for 29 years, a mixture of good, bad and tentative, and in the late years alcohol played a major role for the bad. Even her beloved daughters found her difficult to talk to during her habitual evening drinking. So it was--this was back in the '70s -- that one spring day I took a long walk from our house in Dobbs Ferry (Westchester), and on my way home, pondering my life and future, I found myself saying to myself, "There's only thing more I want out of life, I've done well in my profession, I am a full professor, I have a named chair in surgery. I think I've been a good doctor and an able surgeon. I want just once more to fall in love." I laughed at myself, but believe me, my laugh wasn't merry. Far from it. It was rueful.

And yet...and yet... I guess once in a while, the gods who look over us take the time to look down, and overhear our pleas. At least I believe that's why it was not long after that there was a knock on my door at the Hospital. I opened it and there stood: Solange!

I was not the first surgeon Solange had consulted about her melanoma, a cancerous skin tumor on her thigh. In fact, I think I was the 7th, but this last referral came from Dr. Cushman Haagenson, known world-wide as an expert on cancer, and particularly for his classic textbook on cancer of the breast. He and I were friends and colleagues at Presbyterian Hospital and his opinion was clearly important to Solange. So, as Doctor Number 7, I was chosen and soon enough I was pressured to admit her to the hospital and onto the surgical schedule without delay. The main pressure came from Josephine Hartford (of A&P fame) whose family had donated the Chapel at the hospital She used every device to get the Countess admitted NOW! This was the first time I heard Solange called Countess, but certainly not the last.

Solange's 2nd husband, Jean de la Bruyere, was a legitimate French Count, and Solange used her title freely, before and after I came along, to get the attention of others. Did her title help in getting her into the Hospital? Maybe yes, maybe no. But Josephine Hartford Bryce was one persistent multi-millionaire. And Solange was not exactly unattractive.

The tumor on her upper leg required extensive surgery, but all went well. After ten days recuperation, Solange was discharged from the hospital. At the same time, I was scheduled to attend a surgical conference in Chicago, and that left Solange in the hands of a junior colleague, Paul Logerfo. I wasn't worried about her condition, but the second night I was away, Paul called to say Solange was complaining about severe pain in the operation area. "Should I make a house call?", Paul asked.

Well, in behalf of safety, I agreed that he should. About three hours later he called back with reassuring news. Her wound was healing cleanly, and there was no obvious cause for the pain. "And", Paul went on," I was totally fascinated by her collection of paintings!"

But the next night, there was trouble again. Solange had been feeling pain in her wound, provoking a call to the Surgical resident, and then a visit to the outpatient clinic at Presbyterian. The resident found nothing untoward at the wound site, certainly nothing to be causing Solange's severe pain, but she covered all the bases by calling me in Chicago. I was also perplexed, but believed that hospital admission for observation was justified. I would be back in New York the next day.

When I arrived at her room in the Harkness Pavillion on the following afternoon, Solange didn't look anything like the lovely, well-put-together woman I remembered. She was disheveled, she was wearing no makeup, and all she had on was the unflattering, unstylish hospital johnnie. Before I could examine her wound, I had to briefly check two other patients on the same floor. In ten short minutes I was back in Solange's room, gazing, stunned at the apparition before me. She was still in her johnnie, but she had a red ribbon entwined in her hair, her skin was aglow, and she wore a mischievous smile. I knew beyond question there was no problem with her wound.

I knew just as certainly that Solange and I were in love.

Me, with Harriet's new family

Harriet and Caroline for starts

Eric, older by far than his two sisters but closer as time passed

Brook and Caroline, two years apart

Solange, beautiful but a bit wistful

CHAPTER FIFTEEN

SOLANGE AND ME AND THE VICISSITUDES OF MARRIAGE

(A Bishop to the Rescue. Solange Survives a Dinner of Possible Companions for Me and Introduces her Family in Response.)

The thigh surgery was successful (if one excludes aesthetics) but a year later Solange developed cancer of the breast. By then we had become more than friends, so I didn't operate on her nor did I want to. I got a surgical friend of mine, Philip Wiedel, to do the then-considered necessary surgery, a radical mastectomy. These two operations were in 1975 and 1976. She survived the insults to her physical being, as well as the threats implied by such malignancies. But Solange slipped into a depression while in the hospital and I could tell she needed some non-medical support. I asked her if she would be horrified if I called Paul Moore, then Episcopal Bishop of New York and a long-time friend, to see her.

She assented and Paul agreed to make a hospital visit, but he couldn't quite get the picture. I was still married to Harriet, separated, yes, but our divorce was slow in coming. Harriet couldn't accept my intention to leave her and my daughters. She did her best to degrade Solange and even took the matter up with Bishop Moore by herself. Her activities were vituperative and demeaning. All in all, it was a messy and unhappy year, but I stayed the course. And the more I saw of Solange, the more certain I was that I was at last taking the right steps.

I had been of some help to Paul Moore through the death of his first wife and its sequellae, and I prayed he would help me in return. He kindly obliged. When Paul came to see Solange in the hospital he spent many hours with her ending with a laying on of hands, a part of the confirmation ritual. I believe his visit made a substantial difference in her recovery. When she left the hospital, and I took her to her apartment in the Sovereign, I was ever more madly in love with her.

Finally, I went to Paul and said, "Look, I'm in the process of getting divorced and I want to remarry and the woman I want to marry is Solange." By then he had seen Solange several times and had become very fond of her himself, and she of him.

Paul's response? "Fred, this is no surprise. But the fact that you're divorced and she's a divorcee may be difficult with the Episcopal Church. So here's what I want you to do.. Write me a letter explaining the circumstances of all your prior marital lives."

Hardly a simple task. But I wrote to Paul, the Bishop, and asked that we might be granted permission to remarry. There was no question about our prior experiences at the altar. Solange had been married thrice, I twice, and eager to enter a third. So I sent off my letter, most of it serious, some of it was a little amusing, but I guess I made my case convincingly. So we married. Bishop Paul, of course, officiated. This was on May 31st of 1978, at the Cathedral of St. John the Divine.

A bountiful reception was planned for us at The Dakota, by George Davison Ackley and John Massie. George's mother was a patient of mine, and through her I'd met and became good friends with George. That's why, when Harriet and I split up, and I moved to New York, the ever-thoughtful George arranged a party with a guest list of 14 beauteous and eligible ladies. He knew nothing of my burgeoning relationship with Solange, so I had to tell him I was bringing her along. Since it was too late to change the guest list, Solange became the 15th lady-in-waiting at the dinner. No harm done, Solange charmed everyone, we all had a good time. Solange remained my choice. George remained my friend.

I'd like to mention everyone who attended the elaborate wedding reception planned for that day, but alas, when a re-marriage follows divorces, such in not possible...or even wise. I will report that on my side of the aisle the score was 3 to 2. (Three in favor: Mother and brothers Chris and Eric. And two against: Both my daughters, Caroline and Brooke. On Solange's side, her three children, Mary, Marc and Jacqueline were Pro, and her mother, Mary, and daughter Veronique were Anti. And so it went.).

As we flew away to London, after the elaborate reception, all those If's, And's or Buts were swiftly forgotten as we began our new life. And now, a full

34 years later, I can tell the world, without opposition or contradiction, that our marriage has been wonderful. If anything, it has grown stronger and better as I've grown older. (But somehow, over those same years, Solange hasn't gotten a day older!)

Speaking of my Solange, I'd love to. First of all, she's a three-time Parisian! Here's how that happened:

Her father, Walter Russell Batsell came from a farm family in Paris, Missouri. (The family moved there from Paris, Kentucky.) And, hard to believe, in 1927, her father met and married Solange's mother, Mary, in Paris, France. Ooh, la-la! C'est magnifique!

Despite his rustic roots, Walter Batsell was hardly a man of the soil, like his forbears and descendants. Even in his teens, he was showing an agile mind, with worldly interests His formal education began as an undergraduate at the University of Missouri, at Columbia, followed by a PhD. from Harvard where he developed an abiding interest in all things Russian, especially its economy. Soaking up its culture like a sponge, he became fluent in written and spoken Russian. He was an avid traveler through that vast land, amassing a virtual library of books and photographs. These were the essential tools he used to create endless articles and several books on Mother Russia. His scholarly work was satisfying and well-received, but didn't make him rich. So to support his little family, he set up an investment firm, Batsell & Co. with offices in Paris and London, plus a seat on the New York Stock Exchange.

Solange was born in 1928. In her first seven years, her father was so often away on his financial and academic careers, that there was scant time for those precious father/daughter moments whose memories both haunted and sustained Solange throughout her life. Her splendid father's life was cut short in 1935. What caused his death was uncertain for decades. But recent events have unfolded, suggesting that his otherwise inexplicable death by poison may have been connected to events related to his possible role as a U.S. Counter-Intelligence Agent.

Solange's father's brilliance was easily matched by her mother's. Maybe Mary Batsell's formal schooling fell short of Walter's but she gave herself a first-rate education in contemporary art, much of it self-taught. It certainly didn't hurt that she was a long-time friend of Alexander Calder, whom she met in Cambridge, Massachusetts. Mary's personal collection of paintings and statuary had amazing quality and breadth. Happily for us, much of it is still in Solange's keeping.

Mary Batsell never married after her husband's death, and she and her daughter remained best friends for the rest of her life. Mary had fascinating friends all over America, including New York and California, so Solange went to schools on both coasts, where her quick mind and unquenchable curiosity almost automatically kept her in academic leadership roles. She also took up tennis in Los Angeles, where her tutor was the great Bill Tilden. (Having him as teacher was like a teenager having Joe DiMaggio as a batting coach!) In short, Solange not only survived a restricted family life, but also set herself up for a swiftly arriving college career. And all the while, of course, she was caught up in the glittering whirl of the star-studded society of Hollywood, thanks to her mother's contacts.

Solange and her mother Mary were inseparable. They were deeply bonded to each other and throughout our marriage they were in daily touch, whether in Paris, New York, or even Battenville of upstate New York.

Once again, in the interests of full disclosure, I must admit that Mary Batsell didn't really cotton to me. For her own good reasons, she detested lawyers and doctors, and since I sported an M.D., I came under that unhappy rubric. Based on no evidence, she was convinced that I was responsible for Solange's cancers. (But if you want my own Woolworth analysis, I think Mary feared I was taking her place in her daughter's eyes.) She took a perverse joy in hitting me with her cane whenever I walked by. These days, I like to think those minor blows were actually pats of affection...but who knows? Sadly, my good intentions in gaining her friendship met a little setback one day when I came home from the hospital, and found her there.

ME: "Hello, Mary! How was your day?"

MARY: "None of your damn business, Fred."

Solange assured me that this was a typical French colloquy, but I had my doubts. Anyway, I kept a low profile, kept my questions to myself, and over the years, we got to like each other, or at least maintain a wary truce. Mary's most enduring quality was her total lack of restraint. When she had something to say, there was no holding her back. Her thoughts were right out there for all to hear or see. I'll never forget the afternoon we spent walking on the beach near Ramatuel, a village on the French Riviera, unaware that it was set aside for nudists. We soon encountered a naked man walking toward us and Mary brought her cane up to critical level, waving it threateningly at his nakedness, "You should be ashamed of yourself! An old man like you!" Had he, or for that matter any of the others we saw that day possessed better physiques, Mary's response might have been tempered. But for her, the combination of nudity and ugliness was just too much. And to make things even worse, on the way back, a male windsurfer came racing by atop a huge comber, protected from our view except for a small triangle of transparency in the sail, through which his genitalia alone could be seen. A perfect ending to our jaunt. And how we both laughed...Mary the loudest.

Mary Batsell was a remarkable woman; extra bright, insatiably curious, and always interesting. And, if that's not enough, she really adored Solange. And that's enough for me.

I'll have more, much more to say about Solange in the pages ahead, describing our life together. But not just yet. Solange was just short of 50 when we married. I was 8 years older. Our previous 30 years were spent as differently as you could imagine. Solange with her college and law degrees, her piano prowess, her singing career; her multiple marriages and children. And me, two marriages and children of my own, and my career as a surgeon in New York, and educational work in the Middle East. How odd to think that only her illness could have possibly brought us together. But that's how it happened, and for that, I thank my lucky stars. Every day.

While she was at Bennington College, in Vermont, Solange majored in music, following in the celebrated footsteps of her uncle, Charles Pangera, a Parisian and a world-acclaimed baritone. But it was just like my mercurial Solange to suddenly switch from music to Political Economy! This in turn led to a Master's degree at L'Institur des ScienesPolitique in Paris. And it doesn't stop there. She went on to win a law degree at the Faculty de Droit.

While picking up these academic trophies, she also began her lifelong friendship with Jacqueline Bouvier. It was during Jackie's year abroad from Vassar, and their tight little group included Yusha Auchincloss, Shirley Oakes, and Claude de Renty. (None of this high-spirited group ever dreamed that one of their members would evolve into the nation's most engaging (and haunting) First Lady.

Shortly after her school days, Solange's marriage to Dr. Henri Deschamps coincided with her two-year bout with tuberculosis. She spent months in a sanitarium in Switzerland. The only treatment for TB then was rest and fresh air, neither of which worked. But out of the blue, Solange became an experimental candidate for the new miracle drug, PAS. Her recovery was magically fast. The birth of her first child, Mary, followed quickly on Solange's return to robust health. Henri, her husband, soon earned a reputation as a first-rate cardiologist. (In the small-world department, his advanced studies at Columbia were under Dr. Calvin Plimpton, who was later Chairman, then President, of the American University of Beirut. The same post that I was later appointed to. As I said, it's a small world.)

Solange's first marriage was short-lived. In 1956, Henri Deschamps was legally replaced by Jean de la Bruyere, a full-fledged Count of France. Jean got his MBA from Harvard, where he was roommate of a blue-blooded Scot, Sandy Mactaggart. This entrepreneurial pair lit out from Cambridge to Edmonton, in Alberta, Canada, taking Solange and baby Mary with them. They were in the right place at the right time, since oil had gushed up in Alberta and Edmonton was booming. Both Sandy and Jean accordingly, made their fortunes in real estate, and the wildly popular Countess Solange graced the town and blessed her family with three more offspring; Veronique, Jacqueline, and Marc, in just that order.

When I completed my surgical training in 1954, and was unsure whether to stay at Presbyterian or go elsewhere, I did know that my future would be in academic surgery, so I sought the advice of my chief, George Humphreys. As always, he was helpful. He thought I never would be happy at Columbia unless I first looked at a number of academic centers throughout the country. So Harriet and I, in early 1955, started a countrywide trip by car, stopping at places known to me or introduced to me by Humphreys. These included Charlottesville, Virginia, St. Louis, Chicago, San Francisco, Houston, Dallas, and Philadelphia. We spent two or three days at each site and met many impressive surgeons. But speaking in all frankness, none of the centers struck me as the equal to Columbia, so we headed back to New York and my second home, Presbyterian Hospital.

Solange, no longer wistful

Solange, inseperable from her mother, Mary

CHAPTER SIXTEEN

SURGICAL TRAINING AT COLUMBIA, FROM SOMEWHAT SIMPLE, TO VERY COMPLEX

(Why Surgery Became My Religion. Some Disturbing Thoughts about Today's Surgical Training. Mourning the Closure of the Hospital Wards.)

Was my decision valid? Forty years at Presbyterian Hospital thereafter did nothing but confirm my choice. I couldn't have been happier as I climbed the academic ladder at Columbia, beginning as an assistant professor and ending as a full professor of surgery in the late 1960's. By then I occupied a named chair (Auchincloss Professor of Surgery). Dr. Hugh Auchincloss, after whom the chair was named, had been one of my senior teachers during my training, a remarkably interesting and bizarre man. He introduced several new techniques involving the surgery of the stomach and breast. This great doctor, when risk was involved, thought nothing of sleeping next to his patient on the ward for the first night or two after surgery. Admirable!

On ward rounds, he became known for his habit of grabbing the necktie of the student or resident being questioned. This was not a popular habit, and one day the house staff on rounds responded with vengeance. The resident, whose necktie was in the hands of Dr. Auchincloss, took a pair of bandage scissors from his pocket and cut the necktie off near the knot and all the other residents followed suit, cutting off their ties. A childish maneuver, you may say, but it worked! The next day, on rounds, Dr. Auchincloss produced a new necktie for all concerned, to their cheers, and never again did he tempt fate. He was a good man, innovative and caring, and his son, Hugh, Jr., became one of my close friends. (When Hugh, Sr. retired, his colleagues, family, friends and parents raised the funds to create a professorial chair, and I was the happy first one to occupy it.)

Although my teaching involved all aspects of surgery (excepting brain and heart and lungs) my particular interest was in the cancer of the abdominal organs, the breast and the skin (melanoma). I was involved in research projects as well, most often dealing with new areas of chemotherapy in the treatment of malignancies. So the days were full and satisfying and I loved every minute of them.

Did I make any advances in the surgical field? The answer is no, despite my involvement in research trials of varying sorts. Were my surgical skills worthy of mention? Some would say yes, (I did receive awards for such excellence from both Columbia and New York Presbyterian, and I won't take issue with them), but my ambition was always to be known as a good doctor who cared for his patients and treated them with compassion at the bedside and with skill in the operating room. For me, these characteristics are what comprise good teaching, and I would be happy to think I was both, a good doctor and a good teacher – a role model for students and surgical trainees.

But, but, but! What in the world was it about surgery that grabbed me and held me in thrall for over 30 years? Indeed, if it wasn't for the mandatory retirement age of 65 that Columbia strictly upheld, I daresay I'd still be scrubbing up for my next operation. That absurd rule did change shortly after I retired. Thank goodness! 65 is a ridiculously young age to block any surgeon, with years of skills and judgment, from operating, so long as they have their wits (and their hands) about them.

But back to the opening question: What was the magic, the satisfaction, the allure that drew me to the operating room, day after day, year after year? To a non-surgeon it must sound boring to the point of madness. Performing the same surgeries, for the same maladies, patient after patient, in an unending procession. Well, at least for this surgeon, the answer is simple:

No two operations, no matter what their title, are ever duplicates of one another. Patients are unpredictable, different, and endlessly fascinating. In their anatomy, their age, and of course, their health. Also, the pathology of each disease you are treating has a myriad of different presentations, each with its subtle anomalies, some simple, others immensely more complex.,

And therein lies the challenge, always calling for seasoned judgment, and beyond that, precise surgical skills. Which is why the young surgeon-to-be may feel nervous or fatigued or uncertain, but is never bored, and making that incision never becomes routine.

Speaking for myself, there is an incomparable joy in performing well in the operating room, completing a complex procedure, knowing that the job was well done. For me, this could often lead to song. These days, many surgeons have music piped into the O.R. as they work. I still prefer to march to my own drummer…or fife, regardless of the quality of my voice.

I loved…dearly loved…my years in the Department of Surgery at Presbyterian Hospital.

But the seven years of training following my stint in the Army Medical Corps, were, to me, the most memorable. Because by then I was totally immersed in the hands-on care of surgical patients from the surgical wards. Almost all my surgical education now came from the older and more experienced residents on the house staff. Hardly a day went passed without either activity in the operating room, or decision-making on the wards. This was heady involvement for a young surgeon, but always available, on the wards or in the OR, were the skilled and experienced surgeons from the teaching faculty who were called 'Attendings'. There was certainly no shortage of patients to learn from, and a surfeit of wise teachers to guide us at all levels. And to think I was also being paid! $63 a month! And on top of all that, meals at the hospital were free, and so was our lodging in the hospital. Of course, as my years of residency training passed, my stipend increased annually. But even as a full professor, my maximum salary was only $34,000. Later on, as I set up my private practice, my patient fees eased the financial situation considerably.

"We were nurtured well in our years of training.", I noted in our book 'A Proud Heritage'. (It was written by Fred Jaretzki, Ken Forde and me, in 2003) "Teaching then was never by rote. Our teachers were many and each had his own singular modus operandi at the bedside or in the operating room. This prepared us well for the real world of Surgery. We learned there was more than one way of doing things, and as senior residents we were expected to be able to defend our choice amongst treatment options. The occasional mistakes and misjudgments of others, as well as our own, were conceded and discussed in open forum."

"The atmosphere in which we worked was warmly collegial. We were friends, not competitors, and there was a willingness to help one another out, overworked and underslept as we were. We labored together, shared the same dreams, and despite the challenges and demanding workload, we took joy from it. I don't remember a happier time in my young life. I had a love affair with Presbyterian Hospital and its surgical service. My heart beat faster each morning as I made my way up to168th Street. The passion faded as life in the hospital gradually became more complex and regulated…but it has never left me.

Our surgical training was largely built around two elements:

First: The dependable availability of non-paying surgical patients from the hospital wards (without which no meaningful training could exist)

Second: The deliberate progression toward independence of the house staff, weaning us from supervision in matters of judgment, and even in operating room procedures.

But our hard-won freedom of action was hardly absolute—because always, the 'Attendings' had the ultimate responsibility for the fortunes of the patients on their assigned public wards. And oh, how well that system worked for all concerned.

Think of it. The confidence we gained as surgeons-in-training, was always tempered by the sage advice and experience of the 'Attendings' How lucky we were to have such concerned overseers and teachers. For the most part, they paid attention to our opinion when decisions about patient care were on the table. Even when that table was the operating table! And most times in the awesome permission to use the scalpel. But always, and importantly, the Attendings' were reassuringly at our shoulders, ready to step in at the critical moment their help was called for.

That we were performing surgery on fellow human beings, often unassisted, while still in training, bothered us little. The occupants of the surgical wards in Presbyterian, our patients, were for the most part, unquestioning of our judgment, and, just as today passengers put their trust in the skill of the jet liner pilot, so patients were almost nonchalant in their acceptance of the surgeon's almost priestly and unchallenged role After all, at the bedside we were their friends and even their saviors. But in the operating room, for the most part, they were confident knowing that a familiar team of competent young surgeons was at work on their behalf.

We were rarely asked the name of the surgeon in charge in the OR, nor did we ever feel the need to identify him. Even so, some of the surgeons-in-training (myself included) felt uncomfortable withholding anything from our patients, and we decided to be open and above-board about our training system. Well, wasn't I delighted to find that almost every patient we came clean with both understood and appreciated our candor. (Those few who objected were guaranteed a surgeon of their choice.)

Serious problems in surgical training arose when Presbyterian Hospital, driven by economic needs, closed our beloved wards (and patients) and replaced them with semi-private rooms, now occupied with the patients of doctors in private practice. Paying patients! This modern switch was designed to meet the burgeoning financial needs of the Hospital, but very little thought was given to the drastic effects on surgical training that would inevitably ensue.

Were the liberties heretofore given to the house staff during the 'ward period' to be scuppered entirely? Were these semi-private patients going to insist on being treated only by fully trained doctors, especially in the operating room? Was decision-making regarding patient care to become the exclusive property of the private and semi-private caste?

These are proper questions, and they naturally lead to other fears just as pertinent. The answers are still in the making. When the new system was put into place, we, the surgeons-in-training, were no longer on the house staff, but were suddenly full-fledged 'Attendings', with responsibilities to match. So the question of surgical training was ours to contend with, and our answers were equivocal, at best. Total honesty between patient and doctor was insisted on. The patient was to be told the identity of his caregiver, in the OR or out, and the role of the surgeons-in-training was to be explained in full. And that included their function during surgery. Wait a minute! Should the trainee be given the scalpel? Well, yes, but only for those steps of an operation that fell within his grasp. At first, for example, only the opening or closing of the initial wound. As time (and experience) passed, the trainee would gradually advance to doing a more complex part of, or even the entire operation. But always under the watchful eye of the attending Surgeon, who was always ready to step in.

During these times, others pitched in. The New York Times sent their health columnist, Jane Brody, to find some answers by interviewing me at New

York Presbyterian. That she did, and wrote a column titled 'Ghost Surgery'. It created quite a stir, especially in the surgical community, where involving residents in private-patient care was recognized as a crucial adjunct to resident training. And this contentious issue still swirls about us today, mostly as a conflict between 'Patient's Rights' and 'Surgical Training'. Not surprisingly, and perhaps for the best, it has resulted in institutional and governmental regulations that favor the patients. For one example, the workweek of the hard-pressed resident is now limited to 80 hours, hopefully to prevent mishaps due to doctor-fatigue. There is also a mandatory requirement of Attendings supervision of resident participation in the O.R., especially during the main segment of all surgical procedures. That is now the law.

While I'm persuaded that such changes are justified, the jury is still out on whether they actually benefit the patient. Surgical training has certainly suffered. Even more important than the loss of resident independence has been the progressive depersonalization of doctor/patient relationship during recent years. Once considered a central component of effective medical care. Much of this was brought about by the ever-shortened hospital stays, and the associated 'same-day' surgery, both of which severely limited the chance for residents-in-training (and surgeons-at-large) to know their patients as we once did.

I really hate to see surgery become a purely technical exercise. But it's inexorably headed in that direction, even including, these days, the use of robotic surgery. It makes me take a longing look backward, to a half-century ago, to the days when personal relationships were the joy and satisfaction of our particular profession.

I use the adjective 'particular' on purpose, because I'm reasonably certain that there will never be a simple solution to the myriad problems associated with surgical education. But that bothers me little. For all that is within me knows that surgeons will always find a way to inculcate care and skills in the operating room, however difficult the challenge. And, beyond a peradventure of a doubt, care of the patient will forever remain our irreplaceable goal.

CHAPTER SEVENTEEN

A TALE OF TWO PATIENTS: WITH A WORLD OF DIFFERENCE

(The Case of the Missing Needle. My Triumphant Day in Court. Followed by a Near-Catastrophe which Shaped My Future.)

Whatever the validity of my thoughts about surgical training, I was indeed happy in my work, particularly for the challenging problems each day brought among new and old patients. Some are worth recalling:

One day I was confronted with two new emergency admissions, both patients hemorrhaging from the upper gastrointestinal tract and both requiring immediate surgery.. One was a young man of 20, the other an alcoholic middle-aged Irishman, and the cause of bleeding in both was a peptic ulcer of the lower stomach (duodenum). Surgery went well in both, but in sewing up the wound of the obese Irishman, Pierce Cavanagh, the last stitch taken in the deep abdominal fascia resulted in a broken needle. Try as I might, I couldn't locate the needle tip in the wound; even a magnetic locator failed to help. So I finally X-Rayed the area and again found nothing. I wasn't overly concerned; needles are broken daily and almost never cause problems. The negative X-Ray made it almost certain that the needle was somewhere else in the operating room, but not in the wound.

Both patients had uneventful post-operative courses. But I was curious about one thing, namely, what would cause a peptic ulcer in an otherwise healthy young man. I put the question to him, and at first he was unresponsive, strangely so. But finally the truth emerged, with tears. He had been born of an American father and a Spanish mother in Barcelona, Spain. She, the mother, came from a traditional and strictly observant Catholic family, and when the father, a businessman, was called back to America, he took his family with him, including his ten-year-old son. Before embarking from Spain, the mother, following a Church dictum, affianced her boy to two daughters of a friendly

Spanish family, on the condition that he was to marry the daughter of his choosing before his 21st year. Put yourself in his shoes! He hadn't been back to Spain for ten years, he remembered nothing of the family involved, particularly the daughters, he had but four months left in his 20th year, and his mother was adamant about his obligation. As he left the hospital, I wished him the best and he promised to let me know about his forthcoming venture to Spain.

Six weeks later a letter arrived from Barcelona. "Dear Doc" it began, "I took the slowest possible means of transportation to Barcelona, many times considering reneging on my duty , but I finally arrived at my destination. The entrance to the impressive house was gated, but shortly after I rang the bell a young girl of striking beauty opened the gate and led me up to the house. You won't believe it, but the older second daughter was of even greater beauty! The parents welcomed me warmly, and for over two weeks I alternated between the two girls for an evening out, but always with a chaperone. My decision was finally made for the younger daughter, and on day 17 there was at last no chaperone! I can't possibly tell you how happy I am. Our wedding is set for next month, in Barcelona, and I wish you could be here. All my thanks for your support and understanding ".

Epilogue: I heard yearly from them – they now have three children, and sound happier than ever. And I have added an extra thought to my concepts about marriage!

The other case of interest, the Irishman, Pierce Cavanagh, took a different course. After his discharge from the hospital, he returned to my office frequently, not for any medical reason, but because he wanted to tell me how much he loved me, and appreciated my care. Most times he was clearly under the influence, but one day, perhaps two years later, he arrived sober, and serious – hardly the Pierce Cavanagh I knew – and told me of his recent visit to a neighborhood doctor because of abdominal pain. An X-Ray taken in that doctor's office suite turned up the long- lost broken needle tip. I was amazed, and immediately reviewed the film I had taken in the operating room. On careful examination I found that elusive needle tip. The X-Ray had caught it end on and it was barely visible. My patient was upset, and so was his wife who complained that his alcohol consumption had doubled as a result. What could I do but end these complaints once and for all, by removing the damned needle.

I admitted Pierce to the hospital and under local anesthesia , removed the foreign body in about twenty minutes.

But did that end the problem? Not by a long sight. A month or two later I received, from a legal firm, an accusation of malpractice for having left a broken needle in the wound, thus causing intolerable and persisting pain. The lawyers in Presbyterian Hospital, invoking the term "re ipse loquitor" (it speaks for itself) advised me to settle the suit out of court.

"Like hell!", I decided. I was not guilty of malpractice and was unwilling to compromise, so I found myself in court in lower Manhattan ready to do battle "for the right". The judge was an experienced female, but not without prejudices, and when she called me into her chambers after a morning of severe examination, she laid it all out. "You've come down from your lofty institution behaving like a knight on a white horse," she said. And added "I have nothing but negative things to say about doctors; they almost killed my father. But I was privy to the meeting you had with your patient this morning and I know you're not guilty of malpractice".

She had seen Pierce's distress when he saw me in court. He had broken into tears, and as he crossed the courtroom towards me, blurted out for everyone to hear, "Oh doctor, my doctor, they promised me that you would not have to go to court!"

His tears continued as he was led back to his seat. But there was silence in the room; everyone there, including judge and jury, had heard the outburst, and were moved. And later, in the chambers with Pierce after lunch, the judge called in the lawyer for the prosecution, and glared at him. "You're a disgrace to your profession. Ordinarily I would support a settlement of five thousand dollars in behalf of Mr.Cavanagh. Now I will disallow any more than one thousand, and this to be paid for his day of hospitalization. And you, you sonofabitch, if I ever see you in this court again, I will see that you are disbarred!"

My patient Pierce and I embraced, the judge and I shook hands, and I went home, duly sobered and without my white horse. I never saw Pierce again. I'm afraid he was so chagrinned by his part in my court appearance that he couldn't face me again. This made me very sad. I missed him.

Looking back over my half-century of surgery, I still remember, with undiluted rue, a case where the near-fatal results were entirely the results of my doing. The patient was an elderly Latino woman from Washington Heights. She spoke no English, so her children explained her troubles. An examination quickly made the diagnosis obvious. It was clear that her pelvic pain was caused by nothing serious. A local injection of an anesthetic would make a digital rectal dilatation possible and her problem would be over with. So I scheduled an appointment for this procedure.

On the day in question, I foolishly failed to make certain that the commonly used anesthetic agent was available on the office floor. But it wasn't. So I was forced to leave the patient on the examining table and take the elevator to the Anaesthesia Center on the 14th floor. I found the medication in the equipment room. There was no clerk to sign things in and out (it was lunchtime), so I simply took the agent, intending to legitimize my act later.

I hurried back to my office and administered the injections. Suddenly and unexpectedly, I noticed a change in the patient. She began convulsing, mildly at first, but soon uncontrollably. The attending nurse was monitoring her blood pressure and other vital signs and they were barely discernable. I stopped the treatment and moved up to the patient's head where I could help the nurse. The convulsions had ceased, but to my horror, neither her pulse nor her blood pressure was detectable. Somehow, working with the nurse, we managed to get an anesthesiologist on the run and procure a set of operating instruments for what I deemed necessary, namely, to open her chest and start massaging her heart by hand to get it beating. This we did in a miraculously short time. My tiny office by now was crowded with people trying to help. The anesthesiologist swiftly shoved a tracheal tube in place, even as I had the left chest wide open and had my hand around her flaccid heart. Somehow we managed to push the gurney, with it's parade of helpers and the comatose patient, still kept alive only by hand massage of the exposed heart, out of my office, through the crowded waiting room into the elevator and up to the operating room.

It's a little hard to believe, but by the time we got to the O.R., her heart was beating without any help, her blood pressure was creeping up toward normal, and her outlook was becoming promising. But by then, also, I learned from the anesthesiologist that the drug I had injected into the patient had 'For Topical Use Only' on its nameplate. This warning meant that it had to be applied superficially, not injected into body tissue. So it was inescapably my fault. Mine alone to realize that through my carelessness, my patient might have died. (A painful and lingering irony was this: My patient not only recovered, but the family thought I was God incarnate for saving her life.)

Dr. Humphreys, my Surgical Chairman, took a different view. He knew the entire case. He also felt my guilt and anguish, but he knew exactly the right way to deal with me. He insisted that I report the case, in full, to the entire Department at the weekly meeting. This I did, in painful detail. I remember that some kind souls ventured that my patient's response could have been caused by allergies. But I, and they, knew better. As for myself, if Dr. Humphries thought my public confession would serve as expiation for my sins, he was both right ...and wrong. Because I still have nightmares about that terrible day, and my irresponsible part in it. But I also harbor a conflicting notion: I fully believe that the episode turned me into a better doctor.

CHAPTER EIGHTEEN

LEARNING HOW TO CLOSE

(AND OPEN) THE DISTANCE BETWEEN

DOCTOR AND PATIENT

(The Importance of "Pulling up a Chair." Keeping Emotions at Arm's Length.
A Terminal Patient's Shocking Death.)

Not a day passed during those eye-opening surgical years without learning something new about my abilities…or my failure to fulfill my calling as a doctor. Here are two of them, both small but memorable, one bringing joy, the other, sadness:

Bob Wylie, an outstanding pulmonary surgeon and one of my closest friends on the Columbia faculty, was greatly beloved by his colleagues and his patients. One day I had the temerity to ask him what the secret was behind the extraordinary affection in which he was held.

"That's a silly question, Fred. I'm no different from anybody else on the surgical faculty. I like people. I like what I do. And I have no secrets…well, maybe just a small one. When I make rounds every day, and visit my patients, even for a few moments, I never stand at the door, or at the foot of the bed. I always draw up a chair close to the patient, and talk eye-to-eye, man-to-man, or man-to-woman. It gets rid of 'hospital tension' and adds to the friendship."

I followed Bob's 'secret' from then on, and had no cause to regret it. What a wonderfully human piece of advice!

Equally simple were the informal conversations I had with a sweet and elderly patient on whom I'd performed some serious surgery. I don't recall whether she had husband or children, but she became attached to me, a not unusual reaction of patient to surgeon. Every time she returned for a periodic check-up, she thanked me effusively, saying, as she left, "I love you, Dr. Herter."

And I always responded in the same tone, "Well, of course, I love you too, Mrs. X", never thinking this was anything more than a kindly and commonly used form of 'Goodbye'. But one day I added, in apparent intimacy, "Before you leave, Mrs. X, I want to tell you something I know will make you happy. I am finally getting married again." I looked for her approval. But my mistake, my devastating mistake, was immediately apparent. Her face hardened with hurt and anger, and as she reached the door, she turned and left me with:

"This is the last I will see of you!"

And so it was. I tried without success to reach her by phone and by written message. But to no avail. I never saw her again.

The anguish I had caused this lovely old patient was innocent but inexcusable, and I learned from it to be more cautious and selective with my expressions of affection.

I should mention one further surgical case of mine which I find difficult to forget. I speak not to my abilities or failures, as in the last pages, but to the unspeakable sadness that occasionally accompanies our line of work.

A bright and engaging middle-aged man (name omitted) appeared in my office one day, and on my examination, was found to have a cancer of the rectum. At his request, I left out no details regarding diagnosis, the prognosis, and the necessary surgery required. Cure appeared possible, even probable. But the operation would leave him with a colostomy (a new rectum with the opening situated on his abdomen). He accepted this news with a stoicism rarely seen, and the rest of his visit had us talking as friends, exchanging views on world issues, personal interests, even the pennant chances of the New York Yankees! It turned out that he knew more about my father's political and foreign service activities than I did, and he talked modestly about his own role in the international food business. (I learned later from his friends that he was the Number One in that field in America.

At any rate, his operation was soon done and it went well. I visited him in his private room that very night. His surgery had been almost 3 hours long, and I was amazed to see him sitting up in a chair beside his bed, reading a new book on baseball!. His entire recovery was short and uneventful, and our personal friendship flourished at the same time. I came to know his wife and children, one of whom was a celebrated scientist in California.

Two years later, this remarkable man showed up in my waiting room, this time worried about a lump in his breast. Its form and texture suggested cancer, rare as that is in a male, and soon enough, biopsies confirmed my diagnosis. The operation, a radical mastectomy, disclosed the cancer had spread to the draining lymph nodes and X-Rays found tumor metastases in his lungs. The outlook could not have been more ominous. A trial treatment in which both X-Ray and chemotherapy failed to halt the progression. He soon abandoned his important life's work. Meanwhile, the disease spread to other parts of his body, and, though he seldom complained, it was evident that his suffering was beyond the reach of even the most powerful pain-killers. It became almost impossible for him to come in from Brooklyn for treatment, and he refused hospitalization.

Early one morning I got a call from his wife, with the not unexpected news of his death. After the usual words of condolence, I asked how he had died.

Her answer rocked me.

"He was shot to death by our older son…the scientist from California!"

The son, who had spent a recent visit with his father in New York, was so distraught by his suffering, that he flew back to New York, carrying a loaded pistol, and without any preliminary discussion, had fired two bullets into his father's brain.

Such a story leaves me haunted. How can I reconcile the beginning of my Hippocratic oath: ' First, do no harm.' to my wondering whether I could, or would commit such an act, or wish it to be enacted on me, should I, or one I love, be inflicted with overwhelming and crushing, relentlessly all-consuming pain. It's a point to be considered before we pronounce judgment on Dr. Kerkorian.

Fred and the best of company: fellow surgeons at Columbia-Presbyterian Hospital.
From the left: Doctors Frederic P. Heter, José M. Ferrer, John M. Kinney, Robert H. Wylie, Edward B.
Self, Robert G. Bertsch, Alfred M. Markowitz, Philip D. Wiedel, Milton R. Porter, George H. Humphreys,
Frederic R. Randall, Robert H. E. Elliot, Jr., Harold D. Barker, and Thomas V. Santulli, circa 1967.

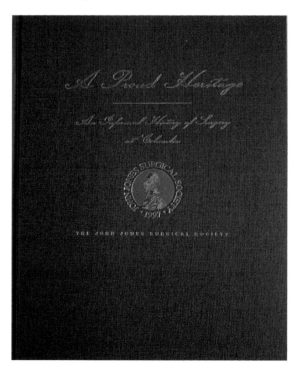

My first book, A Proud Heritage, An Informed History of Surgery at Columbia

CHAPTER NINETEEN

TEACHING SURGERY TO AN OLYMPIC SABER CHAMPION

(Chief of Surgery at Delafield, Hospital. Moving Downtown.
New Ties to the American University of Beirut.)

Being on the faculty at Columbia carried many obligations, aside from surgery. In 1960 I was asked to join the executive committee of the University. William G. McGill was the newly appointed President of Columbia. He was a bright attractive administrator and teacher and I had known him earlier in another capacity. But what faced him in 1968 was yet another student uprising. This one had possibly dangerous qualities. The students took over by force some administrative offices, and the police had been called in. President McGill took charge promptly and 24 hours later was still 'on the bridge', giving orders. But serious fatigue was impinging on his judgment, and some of his orders were unintelligible. I was the only MD on the scene and I tried, without success, to have him rest. 36 hours into the strike he was dead on his feet. His condition deteriorated further , and provost Ted Debary had to assume the lead position. This he did with consummate skill and the revolt quickly ended.

In the mid-60's, I was asked by Dr. Humphreys if I would take over the surgical service at Delafield Hospital, the city-financed but Presbyterian staffed institution a block away. I said yes, and loved the challenge. Delafield catered only to patients with cancer, most of them advanced cases. I learned so much at Delafield about the clinical aspects of cancer and its treatment that it became the core of my own private practice. Both Departments of Surgery and Medicine at Presbyterian Hospital sent residents to Delafield for specialized training in the management of cancer in its many forms. Not only did I teach them when and how to extirpate tumors surgically, in conjunction with their route of spread via the lymphatic system. But I also carried out a number of research projects with them, learning a lot myself along the way.

As an aside, I want to tell you about one of the residents sent over from Presbyterian. He was one of a kind. Not only did he show great promise as a surgeon, but he was also in training for the Olympic saber championship. His name was Bart Nisonson and while scrubbing with him before surgery we talked about his saber fighting.. Our operation that day was a cholecystectomy (gall bladder removal) and I was in the role of teaching assistant. When I passed the scalpel to him, he raised it above his head (a la saber) then brought it down in Olympic fashion to make a perfect incision across the back of my hand! Much blood, but no serious injury, and I helped him through the operation with my right hand only. We laughed about it during his remaining time at Delafield and I subsequently learned that he had not made the Olympics. Too bad. Maybe I had trained him too well

How did our paths cross again and again after 60 years of absence? Why, through our mutual Scottish barber, Jerry Gilfedder, at 72nd Street and Lexington Avenue. Just this past year, I arrived there for a haircut and Jerry said, "You've just come too late. Bart Nisonson was here and he's anxious to see you again." He had become a renowned orthopedic surgeon, concentrating on the knee in particular. As my own problem at the time, and that of Solange, involved our knees, I reached him by phone the next day and to his obvious delight and mine we've been in his hands ever since (without sabers)!

My years at Columbia-Presbyterian were both joyous – and productive. I managed to publish 70 articles in medical journals, I belonged to twenty medical and surgical organizations and was president of the New York Cancer Society and the Society for the Alumni of Presbyterian Hospital. When George Humphreys retired as chairman of the Department of Surgery, in 1970, I was asked to serve as interim chairman of the Department until a permanent chairman could be found. This period lasted two years and I was asked by many, inside and outside the department, to stay on as the permanent chief. This was flattering indeed, but I really didn't want to continue in an administrative position. My love of medicine was kept alive only by taking care of people at a personal level. Since I was only peripherally involved in research, and keenly aware that an academic department should feature solid research, I didn't think I was adequately prepared for a further career as chairman.

So we brought in a distinguished cardiac surgeon and researcher, Keith

Reemtsma, as chairman. He was a graduate of the Presbyterian training program. Later, at Tulane and the University of Utah, he became famous for his work in organ transplantation. His chairmanship at Presbyterian, beginning at the end of 1972, was brilliant, far better than anything I felt myself capable of.

Leaving administration, I gave up my office at the Hospital and shared a private office at 903 Park Avenue with an internist, Jay Meltzer. It was a convenient place to see patients, it had a laboratory on the premises, and I lived within easy walking distance. Moreover, the internists covered each other on weekends, and were familiar with each other's patients. George McCormack, a close friend, was among the best of them. As an aside, Jay Meltzer was not only a superb internist and would-be surgeon, but also an inspired water-colorist, to boot!

This minor move south from Presbyterian to the Park Avenue office didn't mean that I had abandoned teaching or my operating room activities. Far from it. The liberation from administrative duties left me free to both practice surgery, and pursue my research. And my appointment as Trustee of the American University of Beirut, in 1977, opened up some fascinating non-surgical opportunities.

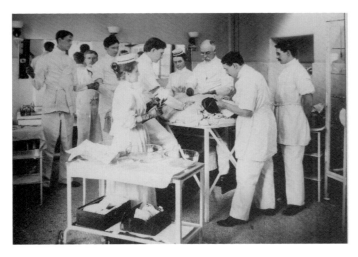

A state of the art O.R., 130 years ago.

My oldest friend and best colleague: Dr Fred Jaretzki

Fred, playing to the Near East

CHAPTER TWENTY

TURNED OUT TO PASTURE
(MUCH, MUCH TOO SOON)

(My Would-be Book, written for Surgical Patients, but Never Finished.
My Love-Affair with AUB. Running a University During a Civil War.)

In 1985, when I was 65 years old, the Department informed me that I must retire. This was no surprise to me. Sixty-five had been the mandatory retirement date for Columbia Faculty for many years and I had already given some thought to what I would do without a remunerative practice and patients to care for. I knew I'd write a book for the lay public because the one thing that had struck me in practice was the ignorance and terror of patients facing surgery. They knew little or nothing about why they were there or what was going to happen to them. And I'm afraid some surgeons perpetuated this fear by shrouding the operating room with almost mystical secrecy. I wanted my book to quell the anxiety of the patient. What was the surgery all about? What were the risks? What should they expect during recovery? Most patients going under the knife were scared to death, and who could blame them? So I plotted out this book, and asked several of my colleagues if they'd write a chapter here or a chapter there. Then I looked around and found a publisher.

She was a very active new person in the game of publishing named Enid Hollingsworth. She worked for Hearst and became excited by my book and its possibilities. She ended up by giving me $100,000 in upfront money to complete the project. So I left my Park Avenue office and started writing. I'd meet Enid from time to time and she'd push me along. But I didn't quite get into the swing of it, because at that time I found myself getting more and more absorbed by the American University of Beirut. That interest, as I've said, began when I was an intern working under Allan Whipple at Columbia. But this interest became focused in 1958 when I got a call from an old Columbia colleague who was the medical dean at AUB, saying that the chairman of surgery at AUB was due for a sabbatical leave. Would I be interested in coming out there and taking over the surgical department in his absence?

Well, I was still married to Harriet and we had two small children at home (my son, Eric, was off at boarding school). Harriet and I talked it over and I obtained the post report from Washington about Lebanon and the Near East. I read it and gave AUB a tentative 'Yes'.

I next went to my surgical chairman at Columbia, George Humphreys, and told him about my offer. I admitted I wanted to accept, but didn't want to be unfair to the department. George, who in addition to his skills as a thoracic surgeon, had missionary interests (in the Far East), responded, loud and clear:

"Oh for god sakes, Fred, you have to do this! It's only a year and you'll learn more about yourself as an academic surgeon than by doing anything else." So I said yes.

At that time, Harriet and I had a house in Dobbs Ferry (Westchester) and we'd made arrangements to sell it to Mike Todd and Liz Taylor, if you can believe it! But the day before we were going to leave I got a call from Beirut saying everything had been called off. "The American marines have landed on the shore amidst a serious altercation between Christians and Muslims, and this is a bad time for you to show up, particularly with your wife and children."

I was disappointed, though as it turned out the altercation was over quickly, the marines had taken charge, and besides, our family plans had already changed.

The next year, 1959, brought a different invitation to come to Beirut. The Chief of the Department of Medicine, (AUB) at this time was Calvin Hastings Plimpton. He had organized an international medical convention (the seventh such at AUB) and he wanted me to give two talks at the meeting and whenever possible take over rounds at the hospital. Cal had been at the Harvard Medical School a year ahead of me, and after several years at Columbia, as a Professor of Medicine, had held the presidency of Amherst for 11 years. He was also the longtime Chairman of the Board of Trustees of the American University of Beirut. So he wore two hats, and did great work in both of them.

This invitation involved spending only two to three weeks in Beirut, and there was absolutely no problem in getting my chairman's okay at Columbia. So off I went, this time without my family. The two weeks extended to three weeks and I learned much about the university. I stayed with the Plimptons, but took ample time to visit much of the country. I quickly fell in love with the AUB, and I just knew it was going to be part of my future. How right I was! In 1977, 18 years after my visit to Beirut and the Plimptons, I was asked to be a Trustee of the university. Do I have to tell you that I jumped at the chance?

I knew little of this American bastion of culture in the Middle East except that it was founded in 1866 by Daniel Bliss, a Protestant minister from Massachusetts. Its student body in 1979 was an officially unknown mixture of 5000 Christians and Muslims. Most importantly, I quickly learned that AUB's survival was based on its freedom from religious or political bias and its open admission policy. To Lebanese and others in the Middle East, AUB was revered, and even loved. Its graduates, as I found when I visited alumni groups throughout the world, were as loyal to their alma mater as any I have ever seen. And amazingly, in all my AUB travels, I never found a graduate who was not gainfully employed. Indeed, the vast majority was actively engaged in important and satisfying work.

Weeks visiting Beirut in 1959 were barely more than a superficial glance at AUB 's history, and even my later years as a Trustee, then as President, failed to fulfill my curiosity about the University and Lebanon. I was certainly absorbed in the civil war, and in keeping AUB alive, even though it meant I had to work out of an office in New York City. Americans were denied entry to Lebanon from 1984 till the mid-nineties. I suspect that I learned more about Cyprus, Syria, Jordan and the Gulf countries during this period, than I did about Beirut and 'the finest educational institute in the Middle East'.

Of course, I didn't absent myself from the AUB during the civil war. Far from it. Three or four times each year I'd venture to sites in the Middle East considered safe by the State Department, frequently taking Solange with me, as well as new and uninformed Trustees. Invariably we'd be joined by groups from AUB… administrative, faculty, and even the student body. My main concern was keeping the doors of the University open, and the faculty in place. Which was easier said than done. Many teachers abandoned Lebanon during the crisis, and some joined the OCP in East Beirut (The Off-Campus Program.) Remarkably, the size of the student body remained constant at about 5000, and no student lives were lost despite the bombardment of shells exploding on the campus.

Most of what I learned about AUB came from David Dodge, a friend and fellow trustee whose ancestry was entwined with the University since its founding in 1866. David's father was President from 1921 to '47, and his mother, Mary, was the granddaughter of Daniel Bliss, the founder of AUB. So when my colleague David was taken prisoner by the Hezbollah in Lebanon during 1982, and kept in solitary confinement for a year, the last three months of which we in Iran, it was not surprising that the University was shocked and disturbed. He was the first American abductee of the civil war, but not the last. At AUB he was heralded for his bravery and leadership. And, as we'll bring up later, Dave was appointed AUB's 13th President.

One interesting note about David's unconquerable mind: For the first month in jail, he had nothing to read or distract himself with, but he finally succeeded in bribing a guard to bring him a pencil and a piece of paper ostensibly to write a letter to his family at home. What did this resourceful man do? He tore the paper into 52 small pieces, and with his pencil, turned them into a deck of cards. He later said that he must have played a million games of solitaire to while away the days and weeks!

As an AUB Trustee, I had taken a trip to Beirut with Solange, my bride-to-be, in 1978. But during the next three years, 1979-82, we traveled as legitimate mates. Although we sensed danger in the streets, springing from serious dissension between the Christian sects and even between the various forms of Muslim belief, there was more attention paid to travel disturbances in the city than to gunfire. This, of course, didn't last.

The first seven years of the Civil War in Lebanon (1975-82) were relatively mild. The citizens in Beirut carried on their usual lives with rare interruption, because they gauged the risks with uncanny skill. American travel to Lebanon was permitted, and the Board of trustees of AUB held their traditional June meetings in Beirut. But there was daily violence in the land. Often we heard gunfire in the streets below as we attended fancy dinners on rooftop restaurants. And I remember a luncheon given by a trustee at his home in the hills of east Beirut; during the main course I suddenly heard a bomb whistling overhead to its destination near the shore. No one even looked up from his plate!

In 1982, the picture changed. Israelis invaded Lebanon, driving the

Shiite population of South Lebanon northward to Beirut, thus altering the demographic nature of the country and adding to its political segmentation. My last trip to Beirut during the Civil War was in 1984. I was there with the board chairman, Najeeb Halaby, and his new wife, Lo Frick, and four or five other trustees. We were determined to protect AUB from the violence around it and we visited several of the militias, both Christian and Muslim and their chieftains, with this in mind, but I'll be damned if I could tell whether we helped or exacerbated the situation.

Later that same year, 1984, disaster again struck the university. Malcolm Kerr, AUB's newly elected president, was assassinated outside the door to his office in College Hall. There were few clues bearing on those responsible; Malcolm was outspoken in his political views (probably too much so in those uneasy times) and his widow Anne (still a trustee) felt that the blame most likely pointed to Christian, not Muslim, sources. This supposition has never been certified. But Malcolm's loss was great, and it was felt far and wide, including the fans of Steve Kerr, Malcolm's son, who was America's celebrated basketball star from the University of Arizona. After Malcolm's death, The U.S. State Department issued an immediate ban on American travel to Lebanon and the AUB administration was faced with a difficult task of finding a presidential candidate willing to serve under such dangerous circumstances.

Although the Israeli dominion in Beirut weakened as its forces retreated, slowly, to the south, internecine violence continued. Shiites, for the first time, began to play a part, though small, in Lebanese politics. Christians and Muslims were largely separated by the so-called Green Line in Beirut, and AUB students in East Beirut had increasing difficulties crossing the line to attend classes in Ras Beirut. So dangerous was this separation that AUB had to greatly enlarge the branch university on the east, mentioned earlier as the OCP (Off Campus Program). The original number of students in this branch was only15, but it rapidly increased to 1,500, most of them Christian with literally no communication between the two campuses.

Violence ratcheted up. During a 13 month period in the late '80s, 23,000 casualties of the war were treated at the AUB Hospital, and it is estimated that over 135,000 lives were lost in the entire 15 year Civil War, most of them Lebanese. Moreover, Syria had to be called in to maintain a modicum of order in Beirut. Soon over 20,000 Syrian troops patrolled the city streets. Although effective initially, they eventually turned into a serious problem in themselves. That's because repeated efforts to return the troops to Syria failed. Rafic Hariri, the assassinated prime minister of Lebanon, was a casualty of this problem. The Israelis, during their departure from Beirut, also played a major role in the violence – the two Palestinian camps in Beirut were butchered at their hands, and the chief military source for these disasters was later declared Prime Minister of Israel. An awful, awful time.

While I was President of the AUB, I tried to create an exchange program linking our faculty and those of two important Israeli universities. This led to several meetings at the White House, in Washington. But anti-Israeli sentiment was high in Lebanon, and the enthusiastic team from Israel eventually backed off, sensing, correctly, that the proposal was premature. I still feel rueful when I think of the enormous dividends such an exchange could have paid. If only in terms of a peaceful resolution of Israeli-Palestinian antipathy. I still hope such efforts will continue, and ultimately, prevail.

At any rate, back in New York, AUB was trying to stabilize its fractured administration. Halaby resigned from the board chairmanship and I was appointed his successor. So the responsibility for finding a new president fell into my hands. Cal Plimpton was my first choice but he already had an interesting job at the US Library of Medicine in Washington. He didn't want to return to New York knowing that the University would have to be administered from a center 5,000 miles away from Beirut. But he kindly gave in (or I wore him down), and he was elected the 10th President of AUB in 1985. He made one stab at reaching Beirut despite the State Department dictum, but got only as far as Damascus.

So our team in New York was headed by me, as Chairman and Plimpton, as President, with Bill Rice and Landry Slade and Eileen O'Connor as strong support. During the next two years Cal and I made several trips to those parts of the Middle East considered safe by the State Department. Larnaca, in Greek Cyprus, we visited frequently, since Lebanon was only 20 minutes away by plane and we could easily tackle AUB problems with representatives from the campus. Damascus and Amman, Jordan, were also on our agenda, the former close enough to Beirut to allow students to come up by bus for lunch in Syria. And we came to know the Gulf countries well. These included Saudi Arabia, Kuwait, Bahrain, Qatar, and the Emirates, all of whom had important representation from Lebanon in their administrations. (It sounds odd, but I must tell you that from 1984 to 1993, including my 6 years as President of AUB, I never once put my foot on Lebanese soil And any visits to Lebanon which did occur never exceeded a week and were always in my role as an AUB Trustee. (One trip returned David Dodge to his beloved Gulf, his first Near East visit since his '82 captivity. It was a joy to share his happiness.)

I was particularly anxious to meet the President of the Emirates, Sheik Nahyan, of Abu Dhabi. I already knew his nephew, also named Nahyan, the Chancellor of the University in Al-Ayn, and he thought his uncle might make a substantial gift to AUB. (The key word here is 'thought'.) So a meeting was set up for me to meet Sheik (President) Nahyan. I was nervous as a cat about such a confrontation. And it didn't help that I discovered at least 20 dignitaries awaiting me in the reception room, along with Sheik Nahyan. I was solemnly ushered to a sofa seat next to the Sheik, while an interpreter knelt on the floor between us. My shaky (or is that Sheik-y?) beginning, properly traditional and courteous, was suddenly interrupted by the interpreter.

"The President wishes to talk to you of something more serious. Namely, what do you think the relationship should be between Man and God."

I looked around for help. There was none. Just a thundering silence. At last my thoughts turned to my mission, and I somehow came up with this reply:

"Sheik Nahyan, I've always thought that education was the most important pathway from Man to God" (Whatever that meant.)

But believe me, I had belted a home run. He looked at me, smiled, and through the interpreter said: "Now we can talk."

We talked, easily and variedly, for 40 minutes. I found the Sheik interesting, responsive, charming, and most of all, informed. That's why it surprised me to learn later on that he had been born in the desert, and had received absolutely no formal education.

My satisfaction with the meeting slowly turned to disappointment when I heard nothing from Sheik Nayan over the next few months. I guess I had expected, if not a gift to the University, at least a word or two of friendship. But this silence gave me the chance to visit him again and talk further, not about

Man and God this time, but about the needs of the AUB.

So nephew Chancellor Nahyan set up another meeting and I took along Calvin Plimpton for moral support. This time we waited for two hours to have the Sheik welcome us, and we also learned the cause for the delay. Yassir Arafat had unexpectedly appeared on the scene, and Nahyan, no friend of Arafat's, was having trouble shaking him loose. But soon enough, the Sheik, Arafat, Plimpton and I were sitting together outside while I tried to excuse ourselves from something that was clearly none of our business. No such luck. The Sheik, thinking perhaps that we'd make a convenient buffer between him and Arafat, insisted that we stay for lunch. And of course, the Sheik's merest whim was law. So there we were, joining about 50 others at the table, me on Arafat's left, the Sheik on his right. For the first few minutes I was the ideal buffer, engaging Arafat with courteous nonsense. But my diplomatic chatter eventually flagged. I glanced about, desperate for help, and espied the hapless Plimpton, 3 or 4 seats to my left. Aha! The answer to my silent prayer.

"And Mr. Arafat, I have brought along my esteemed friend, Dr. Calvin Plimpton, the most renowned educator in America, who is also now serving as President of the University of Beirut. And I know he'd be most happy to address you both."

Happy? Cal gave me a withering look, got to his feet, collected his wits, and began:

"Mr. Arafat, what a pleasure to see you again. The last time we met was last year in Beirut. I had asked to talk to you about arranging protection for the University from the many warring groups in the city. You agreed to a meeting, and when I reached your headquarters, I found myself surrounded by forty armed members of Fatah. My God, I exclaimed, what a perfect time and place to do me in!"

Suddenly, Arafat, red in the face and spluttering with rage, leapt to his feet, and, it looked as if he was reaching for his pistol. He shouted:

"How dare you say that to me after all the things I did for you...and for your University!"

He raged on in the same vein, for endless minutes. Poor Cal, he sat silent, speechless, and bewildered. I finally cajoled Arafat into doing the same, explaining that Dr. Plimpton was well –known throughout America for his droll humor, and that he meant no more than to get a laugh.

Thus the luncheon ended, laughless and in some disarray. But as we left the dining room, out of the corner of my eye, I was relieved to see Cal and Yassir warily hugging each other. And so international relations were preserved for the moment.

Clearly that moment for discussing AUB and its wants had passed. And so we parted company with Sheik Nahyan, sharing the hope that another visit was in the offing. But Earth has orbited the Sun 25 times since that last encounter, and hope has failed to become reality. Sheik Nahyan and Arafat and Cal Plimpton have all passed on, and Solange and I are eagerly awaiting some great-grandchildren.

In 1987 Cal Plimpton resigned and there I was searching once more for a new president. I was not an active or eager candidate for the job, but I did need a salary then, as my surgical days were over. So when the trustees asked me to switch from chairmanship to the presidency, I accepted. That's when Bob Goheen, former President of Princeton, was appointed chairman. I could not have asked for a better chief . Bob was kind, wise and humorous. He never tried to intervene or outsmart me in my job, competent as he was to do so.

Our trips to the mid-east continued, despite the ban on American travel to Lebanon. At least four times each year Solange and I made our way to areas in the Middle East which the State Department declared safe. Bob Goheen came along occasionally, or perhaps a new Trustee without experience in that part of the world. One time, Solange and I had as companions the newly appointed Director of Development at AUB, Harvard's Nancy Pyle, and a new trustee, Rodney Nichols. Nichols was distinguished both as a physicist, and as the former Provost of Rockefeller Institute. Nancy and Rodney barely knew each other; Nancy had grown children, and it soon became obvious that her ties to a husband back in Boston were tenuous at best. In plain fact, by our third day in the Gulf the patter of after-dark footsteps in the house were impossible to ignore. But they required no explanation, and to our joy, Nancy and Rodney exchanged vows shortly after we returned from Saudi Arabia. They had a glorious ten years together, an interlude for which Solange and I claim total responsibility. But alas, Nancy fell ill from cancer, and, after an agonizing year, she died. This happened 20 years ago, and Rod, a fine, fine man, remains single and accessible, with unabated interest in the affairs of AUB.

There were Alumni branches in all the countries mentioned above, and our purpose in breaking bread with them was to exchange news of the University, and to stimulate fund-raising. This last was not easy. Philanthropy was simply not ingrained into the culture the way it is in America. But gradually the act of giving has become accepted, and today Alumni donations are a dependable segment of AUB's budgetary needs. I had one spectacular luncheon with a possible donor from Northern Lebanon. While hoping, in my wildest dreams, for a routine $500 or $1,000 dollar gift, I landed a cool one million bucks! And later, Solange and I played a major role in raising a $12,000,000 gift from U.S. Ambassador to Bahrain, Charles Hostler. This stunning windfall turned into a new student building on the AUB campus.

Looking back, I'm sure the most difficult country we visited was Saudi Arabia. Particularly its capital, Riyadh. The religious police were out in full force, making certain that women were totally covered except for face and hands, and that men and women should never congregate in public. Solange found this intolerable, and no wonder. Because when we went through customs in Riyadh, her bare ankles drew the attention of the police. Bob Goheen had given her his long overcoat to wear, but even this didn't protect her. Then the customs officers, backed by the religious police, threw everything in her suitcase onto the floor. One of these officious bureaucrats was particularly offensive, and I just boiled over. As I approached him with clenched fists, some alert Americans got between us and pulled me away. Which was lucky, because if I had given him a poke in the jaw, I would have been thrown in jail for God knows how long.

That same night the local alumni from AUB had planned a sizeable party at the best hotel in Riyadh. As the guests arrived, most of them couples, the religious police, to our anger and dismay, separated the men from the women; sequestering the men to the ballroom, the women to the coffee shop. And kept them separated throughout the evening! Bob Goheen and I alternated between the two groups all the night, trying to put a good-humored gloss on the event. But it was impossible to remove the damper on what should have been a festive evening.

The good news is that these ridiculous rules were enforced only in Riyadh, nowhere else in Saudi Arabia, nor in other countries in the Gulf region.

The best thing I did as president of AUB was to establish a deputy president in Beirut, so we could easily talk by phone every day. Ibrahim Salti, an MD endocrinologist at AUB, was chosen over the next two serious candidates and the choice was a good one. Only once did we clash: I learned of a surreptitious plan to retain faculty at AUB during the worst of the fighting when many were leaving for the States or Western Europe; this involved a fund provided by Rafic Hariri, the future Prime Minister, and administered alone or virtually alone by Salti (they were close friends). The university administration at large, including its president, were not privy to the plan and although its purpose was valid and potentially useful in preserving the university's teaching function, its implementation was inexcusably faulty. The selection of recipients for funding should have been open and democratic. Sadly, I had to let Ibrahim Salti go as deputy president. But he was kept on the active faculty as a full professor and established for himself a notable academic reputation. And we maintained a friendship despite these difficulties.

Gulf of Aqaba

Nadia, mule and F.P.H. in Egypt

Solange, looking up to me (I hope)

With Petra, Jordon, in the background

An evening with Lebanese locals

Solange and me, getting to know the Near East

Three presidents of the American University in Beruit: from left, Fred, John Waterbuy, Cal Plimpton

CHAPTER TWENTY-ONE

MY FRIEND, RAFIC HARIRI: SAVIOUR OF LEBANON IN ITS CIVIL WAR

("My fortune? Oh, 15 billion, more or less." From His Limo, to His Jet, to His Yacht. Rafic's Death and Living Monument.)

I'd like to tell you some things about my bountiful friend, Rafic Hariri.

He was killed in a massive explosion on the Beirut waterfront five years ago. Signs pointed strongly to Syria as the culprit, but, despite a continuing investigation, no guilt has yet been established. But what cannot be denied is Hariri's vital importance to Lebanon during its Civil War (1975-90) and its heartening reconstruction afterward. Rafic's vast fortune was, of course, the key to his eventual leadership in his country's rebuilding. I once had the inexcusable temerity to ask him how much he was worth, and his nonchalant answer was quietly tossed off, "Oh, about 15 billion, more or less." This astronomical sum is the more remarkable when you consider his modest beginnings as a teacher in Sidon, in Southern Lebanon. But he soon left teaching behind when he moved to Saudi Arabia. That was when he began his breakthrough work in the enormous construction boom that was transforming the Kingdom. By creating a new basic block of building material, his buildings were both stronger and cheaper. He manufactured these blocks at a cement factory he bought in France. Soon he was involved in every construction project that concerned the royal family. And yet, successful as he was in Saudi Arabia, his lifetime passion was Lebanon. As civil war descended on that land, he settled in Sidon, to the south, where, in the hills to the East, he established an educational center that closely resembled the American University of Beirut. He imported a huge workforce of more than a thousand laborers. Working non-stop, three shifts a day, they swiftly erected a hospital and many university buildings.

It was through this hospital that Solange and I, and a fellow AUB trustee, Ted Van Itallie, came to meet Rafic Hariri. We were returning from a trustee meeting in Beirut when we heard of a celebration being planned for the first baby born in the new hospital. A Hariri cousin was in charge of the hospital and asked if we would like to attend. We accepted on the spot, both in the spirit of the occasion, and on the chance we might meet the already famed Rafic Hariri.

That's how it all began. We spent the day in Sidon as hospital celebrants. Later that night we learned that Rafic, somewhere in the Mediterranean Basin, would like to meet with us the next day. Aware of my schedule, he guaranteed he'd get us to Paris in time for a projected AUB meeting. As good as his word, we were picked up at our Beirut Hotel the next morning and driven to a sizable plane on the tarmac. The Captain and the Vice-Captain Pilot greeted us, and an attractive hostess made us comfortable. There were no other passengers among the many seats, and no word as to where we were going. This total silence was maintained for the first 3 hours of our over-water westward flight, and our questions were un-answered. Only as we descended did I recognize the land below as Sardinia. A limousine awaited to escort us to Sardinia's major harbor, a half-hour away. And there stood Rafic Hariri, in white shorts and surrounded by a sizable retinue, all assembled on the stern of his enormous yacht. As we were seated comfortably amidst the group, someone asked it we'd like to break the ice with a drink. Solange suggested iced tea, which was a totally exotic beverage in that part of the civilized world. After what seemed hours, a small glass was finally delivered, with appropriate ceremony. By now Rafic was nervously checking his watch, wondering, I guess, if he'd be able to keep his promise to get us to Paris on time.

But there was talk, and we were impressed by our affable host's knowledgeable exchanges. Our transport to France had us at our destination well before the scheduled arrival. (The jet we were in was one of five that Hariri used each day to make certain his important visitors traveled on time and in comfort).

Afterward, we had no trouble getting Rafic to join the board of AUB. And as he took office, he made a more than generous offering to the school. But his constancy in attending board meetings was less than hoped for. Indeed, in all my years at AUB, I can recall only two meetings in which he played an active role. But of course his importance was not in administration, but in education

154

and its support, particularly during the tense days of the civil war when so many of the faculty and students of AUB were leaving Lebanon. The Hariri Foundation, founded in Washington, on which I sat along with a Senator and a former Secretary of State, was essential in distributing Hariri funds and keeping track of expatriot students in the U.S. and in Western Europe. About 100 million dollars were dispersed annually to such Lebanese students during those catastrophic years. A later investigation concluded that Hariri's contribution to education exceeded all others in world history. But enormously successful as it was, there were disappointments.

Many recipients in our country simply disappeared, evading giving us follow-up data. And many recipients failed to make any contribution to Lebanon or to AUB. But despite these defects, Hariri's name became known, world-wide, and was the basis for his election as Prime Minister of Lebanon when the Israeli occupation of Lebanon began. In 1982, a tragedy: the splendid educational center Rafic had built in Sidon was bombed into oblivion.

The population of Southern Lebanon, mostly Shiite, was forced northward to Beirut, and in time attained some political recognition. Meanwhile, Hariri strengthened his political future by putting vast sums of money into reconstruction. He also provided some safety to Beirut commerce. By importing 20,000- Syrian troops for police duty in Beirut, he helped restore order to the city, but following the civil war, returning these troops to Syria was delayed indefinitely. This became a major issue, one that Prime Minister Hariri had to face. His efforts to reduce the Syrian presence in Beirut almost certainly played a part in his assassination five years ago. But the reconstruction of Beirut remains a living monument to Rafic Hariri. And his dreams for Lebanon are now being lived out by his son, who recently served as Prime Minister.

Somehow AUB survived the Civil War. The faculty was seriously depleted, particularly its foreign elements, but its doors were never shut. Eighty-five bombs landed on campus, inadvertently, we think, and largely on its periphery, where Syrian batteries were situated for their own safety. There were no student casualties, and the enrollment of 5,000 was maintained, a minor miracle given the separation of the Christian and Muslim elements and the escalating violence. The fact is that AUB was, and remains respected, even beloved, by virtually all segments of Lebanese society. Its basic security stems from its traditional freedom of belief and expression. For me, the high point of my time with AUB was the day that the students at the OCP (Off Campus Program) crossed the Green Line from the east and rejoined those in the main campus in Ras Beirut. This was in 1988. It was thrilling to hear reports of the sheer joy echoing on both sides as the University was re-united. 60 OCP students crossed the Green Line without incident on the first day after the AUB invitation for re-unification appeared in the public press. And although the figures are unavailable, very few remained at OCP by the end of the week. For AUB it was the turning point of the war.

For reasons that are still somewhat foggy, the Civil War was declared ended in early 1991, and in November of that year, at New York's Waldorf Astoria, AUB celebrated its 125th anniversary. It was huge affair. The First Lady of Lebanon spoke, well but lengthily; the third son of US president Bush followed, and well into the night. Senator George Mitchell from Maine, whose mother was Lebanese, completed the agenda. But it was a sad event as well. Because the night before, I received word that College Hall, the architectural and administrative center of AUB, along with the adjacent library, had been irreparably destroyed by a car bomb. I relayed this news to the trustees during the night, and we held a breakfast meeting to decide whether to cancel or proceed with the anniversary affair.

Thankfully, the vote was yes, to proceed, and the initial address of the evening was mine. By that time, most of the audience was aware of the tragedy, but I declared, loud and clear, that College Hall would be restored in its entirety. And that every penny to pay for it would be raised in a worldwide campaign. The evening ended in a wonderfully high and positive note. And today I can add that a larger, vastly more efficient replica of College Hall is proudly in place, shining brightly over the University.

CHAPTER TWENTY-TWO

MINISTERING TO THE DIVINE
AT ST. JOHN THE DIVINE

(Opening the Cathedral Doors and Bringing it to Life.
Meeting Stephen Chinlund, A Priest for All Seasons. A Book about Surgery at
Columbia was published, amidst Friendly Fights to Complete it.)

I retired from the presidency of AUB in 1993. I was then 72 and I felt the position should go to a younger man. One, I hoped, who could soon be allowed to live on campus. Two of the trustees had their eyes on a possible candidate, a professor of Near East studies at Smith College named Haddad. After a proper vetting by the search committee, Haddad was named the 12th President of AUB, and moved into my office on 51st Street. American travel to Lebanon was not yet allowed and the following year Haddad took two or three short trips to Beirut. Soon visits became longer and more frequent. But the new president, however bright and well intentioned, was having difficulties in his personal relationships, both on campus and back here in New York. Finally, the trustees relieved him of his post.

David Dodge, whom you'll remember as the first AUB abductee during the Civil War, was then working at Princeton and he was asked to assume the interim presidency of AUB. He accepted, to everyone's delight, and he did such a superb job during his first year that the trustees granted him the full title. So David became AUB's 13th President.

He was followed by John Waterbury, a Princeton professor and Near East scholar. He served for 10 years as AUB's 14th President, and he deserves full credit for restoring AUB's unchallenged reputation as the top university in the Middle East. The student body rose to almost 7,500 and the faculty to 650. The University budget, slightly over $30 million yearly in my term, grew to $300 million under Waterbury. A new business school was introduced, now drawing over 1,000 students yearly, and several PhD programs were added. Waterbury's was a spectacular performance, and his successor, Peter Dorman, appears to be at least a match for him. Furthermore, and strange as it may seem, two recent Presidents of AUB, the 13th (Dodge) and the 15th (Dorman), can each claim AUB's founder, Daniel Bliss, as a great-grandfather! Meanwhile, the 11th president (yours truly) has retreated to a life of relative ease, but retains his seat on the AUB board, and still handles other, less pressing, responsibilities nearer to home.

I became involved in the work of the Cathedral of St. John the Divine in New York, and joined that board. The Episcopal Bishop, my friend Paul Moore, who officiated at my marriage to Solange in 1978, joined his Dean of Cathedral, James Morton, in opening the doors of the cathedral to a wide variety of celebrants and activities. It became a truly living church, out to the dismay and consternation of some of the parishioners, our outspoken Bishop occasionally used the bully pulpit to advance some of his political views.

I came to befriend one of the Episcopal ministers at the cathedral. He had taken on the directorship of the Episcopal Social Services of New York City some four years earlier, and he invited me to join his board. I accepted instantly, for I found Stephen Chinlund, the Director, to be one of the finest hands-on Christians I had ever encountered. The ESS was founded in the early 19th century and had an impressive record among social agencies in this City. Its yearly budget was $14 million, most of the it coming from the City, and it ran countless educational and social activities, largely in the Bronx. The last one, a school for children three years and younger, carries the name of Paul Moore.

Steve Chinlund has passions other than his marvelous wife, Caroline, and his faith. He's an avid watercolorist, and every Thursday morning holds life classes attracting 10 to 12 artists at the Century Association. He's also earned an enviable reputation as a procurer of beautiful female models. His summer vacations are invariably in Italy or France, painting watercolors that are later shown at the Century and other centers in Manhattan. He was one of President Obama's most active advocates in 2008, and he spent several days on the campaign trail outside of New York. Of greater import, I believe, was his involvement with the prisons of New York State, and his extraordinary efforts to prepare prisoners for productive lives outside the walls. His book, 'Prison Transformation' published in 2009, is of signal importance because it challenges the traditional punitive role of prisons, urging them to instead concentrate on the reformation of lives.

Steve Chinlund's activities don't end there. For several years, he's worked on a play that examines the love and joy between artists of advanced age. It has undergone many changes in the direction of comedy. The last line hasn't been written, and we're all awaiting the Broadway opening with baited breath...and hope.

The Council on Foreign Relations, at 68th and Park, took up some of my time and should take up more. Several times each week an event of international interest takes place there and my past relationship to AUB secured my membership and presence. One event there, in 2007, was an hour-long talk by the Israeli leader, Netanyahu, in which he succinctly laid to rest any possibility of there ever being a two-state solution to the Israeli-Palestinian entante. The CFR audience was courteous...to a fault; not a single member of that auspicious group rose to counter Netanyahu's convictions, myself included. So the evening ended as blandly as it had begun. Recent events have, if anything, made even clearer that at least one of us should have had the courage to enter the fray. I still feel a little ashamed for sitting there without speaking up.

My other very good reason for visiting the Council? Its home was built and lived in by my Great Uncle Harold Pratt, and that's his portrait right there in the entrance hall.

I was a board member of both the Middle East Society, and of ANERA (American Near East Refugee Aid) in Washington D.C. The non-political interests of ANERA in Palestine, include health, education, water supply, informational technology and even music. Barenboim was an avid supporter of the music school, with its 500 students, centered in Ramallah but with branches in Jerusalem and Bethlehem. And Edward Said of Columbia played an even greater role in behalf of education in that torn society. The music subcommittee of the ANERA board meets monthly in New York, and hours-long telephone conversations are held with the Director of the Ramallah Music Center. Never do our talks touch on the unresolved violence existing between Palestine and Israel. How remarkable that this cultural activity ,music, particularly one involving children, can survive despite such ongoing mayhem!

It gives me hope for the future.

I have no urge to return to surgery, nor, for that matter, have I kept up my license to do so. But more often than you'd think, the phone rings and I'm asked to pass judgment on the skills of a colleague, or what I think of one form of treatment or another. I'm not much help with the latter questions. There are so many new medicines, with their new names and purposes; so many new different technologies involved in diagnosis and treatment that are simply beyond me. But when the questions are straightforward, like: "Is he or she a good doctor?" Well, then I can help out. Because to me that query usually means, "Will this doctor treat me with concern and care?"

Some years back, I involved myself in the creation of a new surgical society at Columbia; the John Jones Surgical Society. (Over two centuries ago, John Jones was Columbia's first full Professor of Surgery, active during the French and Indian Wars). This stimulated me to begin a book designed to be of historical value to Columbia. I collared a couple of surgical friends, Alfred Jaretzki lll, and Kenneth Forde, to join me as co-editors. And four busy years later, it was published!

"A PROUD HERITAGE: AN INFORMAL HISTORY OF SURGERY AT COLUMBIA".

It was begun and continued as an act of love, love of the college and of our profession. I never dreamed how much work goes into a book, especially one written with cohorts. How fraught with misconceptions or misunderstandings such an undertaking can be. Most of all, you would never believe how stubbornly difficult my fellow editors were, despite the fact that I was the absolute soul of tact and consideration. Luckily, the bonds of friendship Fred Jaretzki and I formed in medical school were strong enough to endure and even prevail over the stresses of turning out a book. The photographs are engaging, and, on re-reading it, I find that Fred's chapter on me is almost effusive enough. The book is a good job, I feel, and worthy to be in Columbia's annals.

Do Fred and I have plans for another book? Hell, no!

Are we still the closest of friends? Heavens, yes!

To keep my hand in as a Trustee, Solange and I have visited Beirut and the University on four occasions since the mid-nineties. And I very seldom miss the Board Meetings held in New York City. But I wish there could be more visits to Beirut; we still have lots of friends over there at the University.

And I can't forget The Mary Imogene Bassett Hospital of Cooperstown, New York, which has been an affiliate of Columbia since my residency days, and an important one. I'm convinced it is the best rural medical institution in the world. It boasts a superb teaching program (for medical students and residents) plus a notable history of research in organ transplantation. It can even claim a Nobel Prize winner on its past staff!

Almost thirty years ago I was asked to join the board of the Bassett Hospital, and three or four times a year I traveled to Cooperstown for meetings. I always enjoyed those meetings and they kept me on my professional toes. I still have a few friends among the faculty and the last Chairman of the Bassett board, Dr. Thomas Morris, is a close New York colleague. In fact, I played a small part in promoting him to the Chairmanship at Bassett. Tom was a Professor of Medicine at Columbia, an Associate Dean at Columbia, President of Presbyterian Hospital and Chairman of the American University of Beirut's Board. You couldn't find a more erudite and distinguished man. Tom is amazingly effective at whatever he turns his hand to, and his unfailing sense of humor is perhaps his greatest asset,

Here's another 'small world' story. Close to a year ago, my oldest daughter, Caroline (who had a debilitating stroke 3 years before, and had recovered sufficiently to enjoy, with help, a post-Labor Day vacation in Maine this past year) suffered a series of life threatening seizures of undetermined origin. She was taken by ambulance to the hospital in Bar Harbor, then transferred by helicopter to a hospital center in Bangor. Sepsis, arising from a bladder infection, was thought to be the cause of her seizures. But with a swift diagnosis and rapid treatment, she regained consciousness and body function. Hers was a miraculous recovery, thanks to the extraordinary care by the professional staff, headed by Dr. Tom Cassidy, with whom I had several meetings. He was surprisingly young in looks (too young, I thought, to be managing such a critical and complex case) but it soon became apparent that he was not only bright and well-educated, but concerned and caring. My daughter was in good hands.

At our final meeting, he showed up with a wide grin on his face. 'Why the grin?' I asked, "This is hardly the time for laughing." But he then let me in on the joke. His post-graduate training had been at the Mary Imogene Bassett Hospital in Cooperstown, New York. And he'd learned of my 30 years connection, as a Board Member, of that institution.

Hurrah! Remember that name: Tom Cassidy. Later I asked him why he had chosen Bangor, when he had his pick of many other possibilities. His answer: "I grew up on the Maine coast, not far from here, and my family had a 37 foot yawl. Well, salt water sailing was, and is, my greatest passion."

Cheers, once again.

Recently, the New York Times published an article on the Bassett Hospital lauding its salaried (rather than fee-for-service) professional staff and the savings effected by this form of support. I suspect that this salary system will play an increasingly important role in the country, and that Bassett will become a widely known model of success for this approach to medical costs.

Dean Morton of the Cathedral of St. John the Divine, and his wife, Pamela

Fred recieving an award on leaving AUB in 1993

162

Caroline

Beautiful Caroline at age 15

As a publiusher in San Francisco, just as beautiful

CHAPTER TWENTY-THREE

LEARNING HOW TO DRAW THE LINE. (ON CANVAS OR THE O.R.)

(The Day I became a True New Yorker.
Remembering a few Wondrous Places to Live.)

Let's see. What else do I do to keep my surgeon's hands busy? My artistic antecedents played a part in my attempting to paint oils at the 92nd Y, and watercolors at the Academy of Art on 93rd and 5th, under the tutelage of Reeve Schley. At this, I was joined by Solange, and she kept me in good spirits as I stumbled along. At risk of disrupting the domestic tranquility, I believe I have a greater aptitude for painting than my wife. Nevertheless the fact remains that the only product of Reeve's lessons on the wall of our apartment is a painting by Solange; a yellow cab passing the Guggenheim, (at least I think it's a cab, my contributions were of an earthier sort.) A friend of Solange called her one night and told her she'd seen me sitting on a sidewalk, drawing board in hand, and staring into a Victoria's Secret window. "Is Fred OK?", she asked.

So be it. It was fun.

My greater success was in woodwork. I never became a true cabinetmaker, like some of the ancient Pratts. But in upper New York State, and in our farm's locality, I became known for attempting to fashion dining room and cocktail tables. Some of them are passable, I say modestly. And working painstakingly with wood is as close as I can get to the art and joy of surgery. (Isn't it odd that the craft of surgery, which I venerated as a young doctor, is so seldom in my thoughts in recent years?)

These busy days, I'm intent on writing a memoir of the two families (the Herters and the Pratts), which was begun by my older brother, Chris, ten years ago. He died three years ago, which only added to my motivation, and I have all the memorabilia on hand to push on. But it is slow work, and by its very nature, it encourages day-dreaming. So many memories that cause ripples of other memories. And don't forget that Solange and I have seven children between us, and 15 grandchildren. Not a day passes without visitation or telephone communication from or to someone in this category.

Life is full, happily so, but one doesn't reach my age without the sadness of losing family or friends, almost, it seems, on a weekly basis. Beyond that, I fear that I've been remiss in keeping friendships alive, even as work has tapered off, leaving me lots of time to keep in touch, but failing to use the phone enough or initiating joint activities. Or maybe Solange is too fulfilling, or I'm plain lazy, or worst still, maybe I'm uninteresting and just a bore.

Anyway, my theory is that women handle age better than men do, and that 90% of the phone calls or letters we get each day are for Solange. Am I that tiresome? Some time ago, I tried to arrange periodic luncheons or breakfasts with the remnants of my male friends. I had success with four. The lunches are at Vivolo; breakfasts at Three Guys. Both spots are nearby, in the upper East side, in deference to my ailing locomotion. Each is a pleasure, to me most of all. Two of these men I've spoken of earlier—Fred Jaretzki and Steve Chinlund. To these are added Baylis Thomas, a psychologist, a baritone of note, author of two books on the Israeli-Palestine altercation, and fortunate beyond belief in having a bright and beautiful wife, who directs the Chamber Music Society of Lincoln Center.

The last, and newest, of these pals is Jim Lebenthal, of municipal bond fame (and fortune). Jim's humor, his boundless range of knowledge, and his constant concern for others has won him endless friends and fans...and, and believe it or not, his charming new bride of six weeks, whose ageless youth matches his. Betty Landreth Lebenthal also happens to be one of my Solange's closest friends.

One final note: Of these four male friends, only one goes back to college years. The other friendships have had incidental beginnings, for which I count myself lucky.

The beginning of my life story was in Brooklyn, but I can't claim any familiarity with my birthplace. I left Brooklyn when three months old and didn't return to it for 27 years. Boston became the site of my school, college and medical education. But New York has been my home, professionally and otherwise, for 65 plus years, and I have no intention of leaving it now or ever. It is my home and I can justify calling myself a New Yorker. The same goes for my wife, though her mother was French, Solange arrived in New York at the age of seven and for over 75 years of intercontinental schooling and child-raising and career-building, she's always made New York her home-base.

Our life together, Solange's and mine, began in the Dakota on the west side of New York City. That looming and one-of-a-kind building was affordable then, and we bought a sprawling yet comfortable apartment there. It was a gorgeous place that had belonged to the great Metropolitan opera basso, Cesar Siepe, costing us what today might bring, at most, a smallish closet in the basement.

For three years, we rubbed elbows with the likes of John Lennon, Leonard Bernstein, Roberta Flack, Lauren Bacall, Paul Goldberger, and other exciting folk. And the location of the Dakota made it easy for me to travel by express subway to West 168th Street, where I worked at Presbyterian Hospital. Life at the Dakota was a heady existence, even though I never succeeded in getting a shadow of a smile from Lauren Bacall. She was interested only in my dog. But my dog, I'm happy to report, snubbed Lauren as disdainfully as Lauren ignored me. Back when I lived in Dobbs Ferry with Harriet, (Wife # 2) and commuted to Presbyterian Hospital, I seldom ventured south of 168th Street. I had no knowledge of the real city and certainly no love for it.

Solange changed all that. She is a city lover down to her fingertips. The year I spent courting her in New York was not what I expected of my new environment. The streets were dirty, yes. Central Park was an untended mess, yes. And some of the city dwellers were barely close to being human, yes.

But one fine New York day, as I was waiting for the local 7th Avenue Subway to whisk me down from the Presbyterian hospital at 168th Street to our abode at West 72nd Street, I had an epiphany about New York City. As I got up to get on the subway car, my over-filled briefcase burst open and the contents flew in all directions. Everyone stopped, there was an anxious silence, and then...then...I was surrounded by a horde of people picking up papers and refilling my case. The subway doors stayed open until the job was done. I thanked all these strangers profusely, and boarded the local train. But I was overwhelmed to be the object of this mass act of decency, and as the train roared downtown, I revisited my anti-city prejudices, feeling more than a little chagrinned. During the stop on 125th street, I saw the express train arrive across the concrete platform, the doors open and a frazzled looking man get off and head toward me. He was carrying a paper bag. When he saw me, he broke into a grin, his walk became a run, and he handed me the paper bag. He explained that he'd witnessed my accident and, when the local train left the station, saw that some of my items had ended up on the subway tracks. He'd jumped down onto the tracks, rescued the papers, then got on the express, hoping to catch me at 125th Street. Inside the bag were a pack of Chesterfields, two pages from a paper I was writing, and my pocket diary! My god, what a miracle! I hardly had a moment to thank him, shake his hand, get his address... but he was off, heading downtown. I never was able to discover who he was or where he lived, even though I kept my eyes open during every trip, hoping to see him again. I failed, but I can never forget his magnificent (and dangerous) act of kindness. That was the moment I began my love affair with New York And a fierce but lasting love affair it has been.

What drove us out of our spacious apartment in the Dakota, sending us all the way across town to 1 East End Avenue, was the allure of living on the East River. So after three years, we traded what were then fairly seedy parts of Central Park West for the watery vistas of the east side. And the price was right - we sold the Dakota apartment for almost six times what we paid for it.

At first, it was an unending treat to watch the boat traffic on the East River, and we came to know a large number of sizeable vessels that plied that route. But we finally had to admit that, compared with the Dakota, our new home site, originally the home of Winthrop Rockefeller, was bland and boring and far off the main transport lines. We wasted too many hours trying to catch a cab on East End Avenue and I was forced to un-garage my garaged car each day to drive to the Hospital uptown. So, finally surrendering after five long years of missing connections, we were inveigled by a real estate friend to move once again, this time to 57th Street and 1st Avenue.

What a difference! Our new neighborhood was more lively and there were unique restaurants abounding, shopping was within walking distance... but still...but still. Street noise was inescapable, and any interior charm of our building was totally lacking. So when we lucked into a small duplex apartment on 74th Street between Park and Madison, we jumped.

Here we've hunkered down for almost two decades, and we hope never to leave. We're snugged into the 21ˢᵗ and 22ⁿᵈ floors of a friendly, well run building. We have two ample terraces on the south and west, we have exciting open views of the Park and in the evening of the matchless panorama of Manhattan twinkling away to the south . Our home is amazingly quiet, and I like to boast that we have attracted (with a couple of handfuls of seed) as many as 26 doves at a time on the Park-side terrace. You already know, of course, like every red-blooded city-dweller, that the dove is a ground-feeding bird. Hence, the scattered birdseed. (Even Pale Male, Manhattan's celebrated red-tailed hawk, has paid us a visit!)

It is an absolutely idyllic place to live and work, and, when wanderlust hits, we also go to a lovely farm in upstate New York State that invites us on occasional winter week-ends, and for long summertime months. But inevitably, after a long spell away, both Solange and I start longing for the peace and quiet and friends of New York City. The farm in Cambridge, New York, is elegantly situated in the Green Mountains on the Vermont/New York border, and it is there that I keep on with my woodwork. And if it wasn't for the hungry and foraging black bears prowling the forest, I would still have my bee hives and enough honey to make breakfast an event, and to provide gifts to the deserving at Christmastime. Just as we had done in Battenville, twenty minutes to the northwest on the Battenkill River, where, on a gorgeous 80 acre 1779 farm, bought by Solange long before the two of us met, bees buzzed, unbothered by bears, and sizable but elusive trout, Orvis nurtured, challenged all our skills with rod and fly.

Fred's workshop (from whence all these tables)

Fred's skills outside the O.R.

Fred's works in watercolor

An interesting building in Provence

In Chianti, Italy

*The Russian church on the
Rue Daru, Paris*

*Paris – View from Solange's
apartment*

Provence, at the foot of the Luberon mountains   *Parc Monceau – Paris*

Provence, close to St. Martin

Fred's sister Del's works in oil paints

 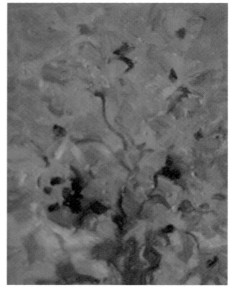

172

CHAPTER TWENTY-FOUR

A LITTLE ABOUT MY KIN, AND A RENEGADE BROTHER-IN-LAW

(My Sister Del Paints Husband Joe Out of a Job. Chris, his Sue One and Sue Two, and Kathy, and 50 Years of Fishing with Younger Brother Miles.)

Our family life today is a busy and bustling one. I have two living siblings; an 85-year-old sister, Adele, and Miles, a brother nine years my junior. My sister, Del, is a recognized painter, a prolific poetess, and probably more lastingly, the founder of "Gardens In Humanity", a rapidly spreading community activity that enlists local citizens to convert junk-filled urban lots into fertile gardens. When possible the surrounding brick walls display murals by neighborhood artists. Del's extraordinary and unquenchable interests jump off the pages of her recent book, Our Sacred Garden, a delightful journey through her poetry, her paintings, and her philosophical musings.

Del's husband, Joseph Seronde, came from an academic background. His father, of French origins, wound up at Yale, teaching French literature. Joe's mother was a member of the famous Shelling musical family, and her father taught the excitement of music to the children of Boston, including a young Fred Herter, each Saturday morning. His eccentric methods included delighting the audience by playing the piano with…an orange, a trick picked up by Chico Marx, and used in his movies. I remember being in the audience for these scintillating lectures. I can't claim that much of what he taught stayed with me (except for my craving for oranges!).

Nor was Joseph Seronde ever diverted from a career in science and medicine. After medical school at Yale, he served as a naval doctor in World War ll. Later, he taught pathology at Columbia's School of Physicians and Surgeon. I knew Joe because of our proximity (I was working in that same New York hospital as a surgeon) and my admiration for him only grew after he married my sister, Del, who had roomed with his sister at Bennington College.

This long prelude begs forgiveness, but it leads to a memorable tale about Joe Seronde. While he was teaching pathology at P&S and doing animal research, he and Del lived across the Hudson in New Jersey. He commuted daily to Presbyterian Hospital in an open coupe, wearing (of course) a beret. He soon became a character in the hospital community. Joe also fueled his offbeat reputation by openly stating his hate for his boss, the Chairman of the Department of Pathology. In particular, he fulminated against the bright young man who was the pet of the Chairman and was being groomed for academic promotion...over Joe. What really bothered Joe was the Chairman's refusal to give him a summer fan to cool his office and his laboratory animals, while allowing this pet of his to refurnish an entire new suite, with the help of professional decorators, and charge every penny to the Department. Joe's tirades certainly enlivened evenings at home. It all came to a head one night, when Del asked if she could go along to the hospital with Joe while he fed his animals. "Of course," Joe said.

"Is it OK if I bring my paints to do some sketching while you're working?"
Again, Joe says, "Of course!"

So, while Joe is feeding his mice, Del is hard at work in the pet's suite, painting every desk, chair, wall, with Italianesque designs and characters. This was akin to Picasso's Blue Period, she explained to the police the next morning when they and officers of the faculty were waiting for Joe to defend his wife's creation. End of story.

Joe, of course, was eventually fired. The Dean's pet, appalled by the way Del's artistry had transformed his offices, kept whining, "Why me? I never said anything about his cute car...or his damned beret. Why me?" And Joe, secretly, was delighted to be leaving the premises, regardless of cause. And Del was just as happy to be departing New Jersey. But mostly, I'll wager, for the imagination and skill she demonstrated in support of her husband.

The two of them joyfully moved to Boston. Soon, Joe found someone to bank his research, and even build a laboratory for him. Del found time to raise five children...even as she continued her painting. And, as I mentioned, she's just published a book covering her many creative skills. It is superb!

About 20 years ago, Adele moved to Sedona, Arizona from Massachusetts, with her research-oriented physician husband,. They built a remarkably attractive house close to Sedona's 'Red' mountains. Four of their five children remain in the Southwest today. The second son, Jacques, became a leader of the Navajo Nation after marrying into that tribe. Adele's two daughters followed in their mother's footsteps and became notable painters. Just this summer, Jeanne, the younger, had her work exhibited in Solange's gallery in Greenwich, New York. And, still more in the small world department, Adele's youngest and biggest son, Pierre (six foot six and the necessary pounds to match) acted as bodyguard for Solange's daughter Mary, when she visited Boston's 'Combat Zone' while at Boston U's School of Journalism . Pierre, our gentle giant, now lives in Santa Fe, New Mexico, where he's in demand as a singer, and successful as a wine importer, while carrying even more impressive measurements than before.

Well, you get the picture. My sister is the matriarch of a remarkable and unconventional family, delighting in artistic creation but even more driven by improving their community and preserving the increasingly fragile world outside it. (Money, as you might guess, is of only secondary interest to this talented and extended tribe of Secondes.)

Miles, my 82 year old younger brother, lives in Manchester, Massachusetts, in his dream-house on the sea, up the coast from Boston, and overlooking Manchester Harbor. He is a Boston fixture, and it would take a major emergency to dislodge him to visit us in NY. The same is true of his wife, Lee - she is a Bostonian with a capital B, as much of a dream as is their house overlooking the sea. She and Miles have four children, Miles Jr. (aka Mike), Dave, Ned and Caroline, and at least a dozen grandchildren (even two great-grandchildren) scattered about - as happy a family as one can imagine.

Both Miles and Lee preferred sports to creative intellectual activities. Not only were they fine athletes themselves; Miles as a letterman in baseball in school and college, and both as golfers of competence (both their fathers had been wedded to the links). And when golf was out of season, they would trek endless miles on weekends to watch one or more of their four children or 11 grandchildren take to the ice or playing fields. Miles, and particularly Lee, seldom missed a sporting event on TV should the offspring agenda be bare, and both could quote endless statistics on the doings of the Red Sox, Patriots, and Bruins.

Their unquenchable and fierce love of sports can still be seen in their children and grandchildren. It is the engine that integrated their family, not just physically and geographically, but with such tight bonds of affection that their family was, and is, the happiest I have ever known. No wonder Miles and Lee are so proud. No wonder they are so loved and revered.

I have never understood how Miles, that staid stockbroker from the Bay State with friends galore and such a family, could, shortly after college, have succumbed to alcohol, but for a short and disastrous while, he did. Then, thanks to a family intervention, he responded promptly, and for more than thirty years he has been abstinent. To this day he attends AA meetings weekly. He's been the leader of the abstention movement in the greater Boston area throughout most of that period. What we miss from his unwillingness to visit New York is made up for by continuing our yearly summer trips to Canada for salmon fishing. Over the past 50 years, Miles and I have missed only three or four such weeks, and our ages aside, we have every intention of at least pondering a trip northward next July. Miles is nice and funny and I love him dearly. You would, too. And, should you have trouble locating him, just try the golf course at the Essex County Club in Manchester. Lee will not be far away.

One last note about Miles: In May of 2011, he was celebrated for his outstanding 30 year leadership, in the care of teen-age victims of alcohol and drug abuse. This is in the Boston area. Over a hundred friends and admirers came to praise Miles, and at the same time, raise $300,000 for him to continue his great work!

The oldest in our family, our brother Chris, died four years ago, at the ago of 89. His background was a lot like mine - Dexter School in Boston, St. Paul's, Harvard College and Law School (the last after two years of active military duty in Europe). But there were differences between us, big differences.

Chris was brighter, he took his education seriously, and he always knew just where he was going, and why he was headed there. Moreover, he had a success with girls, which I envied in the worst way. Or maybe the best way! Above everything else, including the girls, he wanted to emulate our father, both politically and in the foreign service . While working for a white shoe law firm in Boston, he was elected to the Massachusetts House of Representatives and appointed to the Governor's Council. Later he was proposed as a candidate for the Governorship of the State. But his energetic run for the position of Attorney General of Massachusetts failed (he was fighting the invincible Kennedy machine). So he returned to the law, accepting a position with Mobil in New York.

Chris had three children , all by his first wife, Susan. (She eventually became known as Sue l, for reasons you've probably already guessed.) The oldest child, Susan Jamieson, was always Jamie to the family. She married twice, bearing two sons with her first husband, and joined her second, Davis Cherington, in protecting farmland in upstate New York and Vermont. Their work in keeping these lands safe from developers was well-received at the time and remains so today. Jamie's sudden and premature death this past year stunned and grieved us all.

Christian A. Herter III, otherwise known as Kim, arrived two years after Jamie. His life-long interest was not in land protection, but in developing various forms of energy, and providing it for the common good. Maine was, and remains his center of activity. He began his pursuit of alternate energy by converting obsolete river dams into hydroelectric power, at little cost. Other types of energy production followed, and are currently growing under his leadership.

Geoffrey, Chris's third child, took up medicine. (A choice probably stemming from a long period of hospitalization after a serious bicycle accident.) Geoff earned his M.D. at the College of Medicine and Surgery at Columbia. His career expanded quickly, and he's now a highly regarded urologist, practicing in Connecticut.

Chris's first marriage, to Suzanne Celery of Texas, ended in divorce, and their three children had their beginnings in Boston. But Sue One had no love of politics. She was warm and caring and loved life at home with her brood. Chris's second wife, Sue Two, (Susan Cable of Santa Fe and New York), on the other hand, was actively involved in public affairs. Nelson Rockefeller was a friend, and she worked closely with him, to everyone's advantage (including Chris's), when he was in Washington. Now here's a tribute to her delightful presence: Sue Two was adored by the children of Sue one. Sue Two, though, had no children of her own to reciprocate this affection.

But Chris, busy as he was with Mobil's international branch and New

York's Urban League, had his eyes set on Washington. His powerful job at Mobil was soon replaced by one at the State Department, where his expertise in international environmental law was put to good use. At the same time his political horizons were broadened by a round-the-world trip as Assistant to Vice-President Nixon. But elective office was never quite within his grasp. His State Department experience was followed by years of teaching environmental law at SAIS, the Johns Hopkins School of Advanced International Studies in Washington, which, you remember, was founded by Father and Paul Nitze, but now bears (Grrrr!) only Nitze's name.

Chris's late years were devastated by illness. His litany of medical disturbances kept him hospitalized or bed-bound for much of his time. I found myself traveling from New York to Washington every second or third week to keep him company, either alone or along with his third wife, Katherine Hooker. Complaining wasn't part of Chris's makeup. Instead, we talked about lively family matters, political events governing precarious world problems, and, when either the Red Sox or Tiger Woods weren't playing on TV, we might sing some old songs, often ending with misty eyes. I came to know Chris as never before, and our visits were as precious to me as they were to him. He died quietly in September of 2007.

A word (or maybe even a little more) about my children.

Eric, my first-born is now, incredibly, in his 67th year. As I've mentioned earlier, he had some difficult beginnings with Harriet, his stepmother. I tried to alleviate the problem by enrolling him in boarding school (St. Paul's). I thought it might solve things, but in reality, it did little more than separate them. At that time, I hadn't developed the ability that, as a doctor, I later picked up, of being able to put myself into another's shoes, and feel life's problems from the sufferer's perspective. When Eric, during his last boarding school year, decided that Harvard should be put off for a year and possibly be replaced by an institution in Europe, France preferred. That decision won the enthusiastic support of Harriet and me. An educational consultant in New York suggested a new and highly regarded American college in France. Eric seemed pleased by the choice and off he went, eastward, to the banks of the Loire. Going along with him was a classmate from St. Paul's, Dick Jackson. Dick's father was my classmate from St. Paul's. Small world, isn't it?

Eric's very first letters that fall convinced us that the choice was sound. He lived with an elderly lady who was known for the purity of her spoken French. The quality of teaching at the college initially appeared as splendid as the brochures promised. But as time passed, Eric's letters sounded less happy, and by Christmas there were cries for help. Dick Jackson, Sr. got equally disturbing reports from his son, so we decided to make a visit. Together, we went to Tours and discovered total chaos at the chosen American College, where our sons' education was close to nil. But at least the four of us spent three happy days together. At the same time, we arranged to transfer Eric and Dick to a well-known French university nearby.

The remainder of the year was a wild success. Not only did Eric become fluent in French, he also picked up some hint about the opposite sex from the always expert French. And he found the joys of motorcycle touring, leaning into the never-ending corners of the continent. He even survived an attack of hepatitis, with the help of several attractive 'nurses' among his new friends. On the whole, a merry interim year before a return to Harvard, challenged by a new set of classmates.

Eric's college years, fulfilling as they were, weren't exactly distinguished academically. Still, he somehow filled in the voids remaining from that French year, and even topped his old man by being tapped for the Porcellian Club, whose doors he very rarely walked through thereafter. And then, in 1966, like so many other emerging graduates, he faced a world gone a little mad, forcing him into a decision to make about Vietnam.

Despite his inherent opposition to warfare and hence his inclination to leave the US for Canada, he finally gave in to his father's and uncle's pressure and, when drafted, spent a year in Vietnam. Not in actual combat, but by doing photography, and serving to rehabilitate VC's returning from the military front. It was a grievously unhappy year, brightened only by a love affair with a Vietnamese girl. He returned home an inconsolably angry man. From his first-hand experience there, Eric was convinced that the US position on Vietnam was insupportable, and our behavior toward the Vietnamese people reprehensible. Harriet, his stepmother, had nothing positive to say about the Vietnamese people, which enraged Eric further. Looking back, I didn't do much to help. I guess I sensed that his anger sprang both from his unrequited love affair, and our Army's conduct in Vietnam.

Whatever the reasons, Eric found normal home life difficult at best, so he bought himself a third-hand Volkswagen and headed off. Destination unknown; time of return unmentioned. The complexities of the next two years are such that even Eric is fuzzy on the details. We do know his travels took him to Key West, then cross-country to California, then back to New York. and began living with, a girl who fed him drugs, many of them seriously addictive. His cousin, Jacques Seronde, rescued him a year or so later, and helped him say farewell to both the girl and the drugs.

Eric's return to normality involved many: Jacques and the Seronde family in Maine, my mother in Millis, Massachusetts, other Seconded members in Navajo County in Arizona, and myriad friends in California. Initially, Harriet and I played little part in these supportive measures. Eric's post-war anger, his abandonment of house and home, and his infrequent communication thereafter, left us in Dobbs Ferry largely out of the picture. I must confess to keeping Eric at arms length during that troubled period.

The fault was not his alone, and my part was made clear to me by a surgical patient of mine, an aging and wise psychiatrist. He asked me about my family, and he was particularly taken by my descriptions of Eric, who was going through a bleak period, doing carpentry and driving a taxi in California. The day after this talk I received a long letter from Eric, 8 pages in careful longhand. It was our first contact in several weeks, and I mentioned the letter to Dr. Shapiro when I checked in on him during evening rounds.

"May I read it?" he asked, and I brought it to him the next morning. That evening, when I visited him, he seemed unnaturally severe.

"Sit down, Fred," he said, 'and be quiet. I've read Eric's letter...not once... but three times. Fred, didn't you realize that no less than six different times, Eric professes not only his love for you, but cries out his need for you." At this, my throat tightened, and I started to cry. And even today, when I repeat this story, tears come. God bless wise old Dr. Shapiro. From that agonizing moment of recognition, I saw Eric in a totally new light...I felt my soul moving closer to him, and today, every day, Eric and I are inseparable friends. My life is all the richer for it. And so are the lives of many lucky enough to know Eric's warm nature and his creative intelligence.

Our reconciliation not only brought Eric back home. It also focused his energies on measures to end the war. He became a tireless member of the Vietnam Veterans Against the War. This took him to Washington and New York where he worked alongside his old schoolmate, fellow veteran (and future Senator) John Kerry. It was Kerry who asked the awful and unanswerable question of the U.S. Senate:

"How can you ask a young man to be the last American killed in an unjust war."

That question brought Kerry's name to the fore, and positioned him for a run for the Presidency in 1964.

Eric's contributions to ending the Vietnam War were note-worthy. But what brought him the most attention was an article splashed across the front page of the Boston Globe, in 1972. In his beautifully crafted essay, he announced his refusal to pay any portion of his income-tax that went to supporting the war. This proclamation was printed along with a chilling photograph he had taken of two dead Vietnamese children, dragged onto the street by American GIs.

Eric's story drew immediate support country-wide, perhaps more so because the IRS never leveled charges against him.

For myself, I like to think that Eric's eloquent words played a part in hastening the war's end.

You may wonder what became of Eric's love in Vietnam. Communication between them had ceased, but he never stopped looking for ways to be back to where they first met and their friendship turned to love. Vietnam was then off bounds to Americans, and the closest he could get was Thailand. So he took a job there, teaching for the Peace Corps, but this failed to win him entry to Vietnam. Furthermore, the teaching assignment was akin to joining the Thai army. So Eric resigned from the Peace Corps, traveled for eight months throughout Asia, and then returned to America.

Eric didn't set foot on Vietnamese soil for ten long years. By then he had moved to Hawaii, working as the editor of East West Magazine and producing a prize-winning photo-book on the Hawaiian people. From there, working with an agricultural research group in the University of Hawaii, he visited Vietnam three of four times. Then in 1996, he abandoned Hawaii and moved to Vietnam with the hope he'd never leave again. He was still seeking his elusive dream-woman in the Mekong Delta area where he'd served as a military advisor for a year. Failing in his search, he took a job with the Associated Press Television in Hanoi. It was there that he met an attractive photographer named Hoa Tran. Romantic sparks were struck, they fell in love, married and began a family. Solange and I visited Hanoi shortly after the birth of their daughter, Samantha.

Professionally, Eric and Hoa produced two important environmental documentaries on Vietnam. After wrapping up their work there, they settled in Brunswick, Maine. Eric still films political documentaries. Hoa teaches Yoga, while Samantha studies happily in a small private school up the coast from Brunswick. Her performance there bodes well for the future. I keep after Eric to give the world his book on Vietnam. I keep hoping. After all, he writes like a dream, and his take on that foreign policy misadventure would be unique. I'll keep after him, or rather, I kept after him, and now he spends, most days, four hours putting it all down. Cheers!

My older daughter, Caroline, arrived on Planet Earth 11 years after Eric, in 1954. She was always beautiful, she did well in primary school in Dobbs Ferry, New York, and she had, almost from her first steps, danced and carried herself with grace. I was certain that she was headed for a career in ballet. But then, well on her way at 16, one of those uncalled-for life-changing breaks occurred. While rehearsing at the Master's School in Dobbs Ferry, she dislocated her kneecap. This meant surgery. In itself, this wouldn't end a dancing career, but it ended Caroline's desire for one.

Maybe her more eclectic approach to life was presaged by her presidency of the "Kissing Club" in public school prior to Dobbs. I remember that as one of the areas of conflict with me, and her constant battles with her mother, Harriet. My paternal role, as with Eric, was to nurture, as best I could, this avidly curious young mind. So Caroline's acceptance at Colorado College was both a surprise and a joy. She loved the school, she effortlessly made numerous friends, and her eventual career in publishing was forged under the Colorado's remarkable "one-course-at-a-time" curriculum. This unique approach meant that instead of studying 4 or 5 subjects simultaneously, they tackled only one. For example, for an unrelenting three months, they were totally inundated in

History, to the exclusion of everything else. And emerging from that period, they theoretically had a mastery of the subject. Caroline loved that system.

There was also the spectacular Colorado skiing, of course. I'm sure her conquest (and the danger) of the slopes gave her the kinesthetic triumph she had felt in ballet, and helped buttress her terrific streak of independence.

Caroline, not all that enthusiastic about coming back East after graduation in 1975, landed a job with that world-renowned bookstore in Denver, "The Tattered Cover". Clearly, something about the book business clicked with her, and after three years she became an agent for Harper's, covering four states centered in Colorado. She was considered a natural and they soon brought her back to their New York main office. Moving upward and onward, she was lured from Harper's to Scribner's and finally, and happily, to Simon & Schuster. She had a transient battle with cocaine addiction while at S & S, but, typically of Caroline, she cured herself (with a little help from her friends at AA). I can't forget the lunch we had together when her first "clean" year ended. I don't know which of us was prouder. But it's no contest as to which of us was more beautiful.

Caroline's last move (which she didn't take lightly) was to go from New York to Chronicle Books in San Francisco. There she was the number two editor, mastering every aspect of the publishing business, including its politics and personalities. Five years later she took a deep gulp and made the plunge. She began her own publishing house!

Herter Studio opened its doors in San Francisco. Her office was in her apartment, and (with excellent help) she added her personal touch to every facet of book production. She was always on the move, throughout the East, and into Europe. Then, to cap off each year, she taught at a two-week seminar called the 'International Publishing Congress' at Stanford University.

Her personal life was full and fulfilling. She always had several beaux, with one of whom she stopped just short of the altar. She remains to this day unmarried, with more than her share of close friends. I guess the happiest part of her life happens every September when she spends 3-4 weeks at the family sea-side house on Mount Desert Island in Maine. She's usually accompanied by her old publishing friends from New York, and a sprinkling of our eastbound family. This family-friendly house is a happy combination of barn and lobster-shack, designed for Harriet and me by an architect friend, and built on a point on the west coast of Mount Desert. I share its ownership with my two daughters. (Solange is strictly a mountain or city dweller, so, beautiful as it is, we've never spent much time there.) My Eastbound family is a formidable one. There's Miles and his wife, Lee, my sister Del, and my late brother, Chris. Miles contributes 4 children, 13 grandchildren and 2 great-grandchildren, Chris had 3 children, one of whom spends his life on the Maine coast. Del had 5, and they all spend the summer months on Mount Desert Island. Or close by on the Maine coast. Eric, Hoa, and daughter Samantha are settled in Brunswick, Maine, close to Bowdoin College.

Alas, the pattern of Caroline's life changed suddenly about 3 years ago. A stroke paralyzed the left side of her body, and she languished for several weeks in a San Francisco stroke center. Luckily, if I dare use that word, her brain was damaged only in the right hemisphere, so her speech is unimpeded, and her thoughts are clear. She can now walk, with a little help, although her left arm and hand remain unresponsive. But she can read without difficulty, she enjoys TV and the movies, and is contemplating writing a book about the steps of rehabilitation after a stroke, even when those steps don't lead to total recovery. For instance, the fear of falling is constant. Caroline can't be left alone, indoors or out, so two Philippino aides divide her care, and are her main source of companionship. They drive her to medical appointments, and once a week to Sonoma County where she rides a horse...under close supervision...but she's back in the saddle!

Two months ago Caroline's sister Brooke rented a house with her in New Mexico, well to the north of San Diego. The country is spectacular, with miles of riding trails, rivers and reservoirs for kayaking. The neighbors are few but friendly. Caroline was beside herself with joy during this vacation, and on leaving she was determined to return repeatedly. And this she has done,, bringing along her friends from the publishing world. She always comes back with tales of venturesome days on horseback, and serious thoughts of a permanent move there from San Francisco.

To say that Caroline has courage is an understatement. Last summer, we heard from Maine that she had gotten herself into a sea-going kayak, and with a new-fangled one-handed paddle actually propelled herself some distance

185

into the bay! And add to that her stories of endless rides on horseback, accomplished with only one fully usable leg and impaired balance from a deadened shoulder and arm. Amazing! Bravo, Caroline. And keep up the good fight. Along with all our love, always.

My youngest, Brooke, had her 55th birthday two months ago (October 11, 2011). Where her name came from I can't remember, but I liked it then and like it even more now. Two years younger than Caroline, she was quite different in temperament. Quiet, reserved, undemonstrative, easy to live with, Brooke breezed through school in Dobbs Ferry, both public and private, without difficulty. Her friends were few, but close. Boys held little interest for her. She had a marked talent for the piano, and I'll never forget the Chopin Nocturne she played before the school community, plus family and friends at the yearly Spring concert. The beginning was, to me, breathtaking, her touch was sure, and her mastery of musical nuance a tribute to the composer. But then, from the stage, utter silence. Brooke had forgotten the next measures and her agony at the piano was transmitted to the audience. One second passed, then two, then an endless ten, without a sound. Brook arose, expressionless, and with great dignity, walked off the stage.

The audience, not quite knowing what to do next, remained silent. They just sat there, suffering on Brooke's behalf. Next, without intervention of any kind, Brooke stepped back onto the stage, sat down at the piano, smiled to the audience, picked up at the note she left off on, and carried on faultlessly through the closing chords.

Can you imagine the cheers that turned into a roar as the crowd jumped to its feet, in tumultuous ovation. And the proudest member in that concert hall was her father. (Brooke also played a remarkable Petit Prince of St. Exupery that spring, perhaps not to standing cheers, but at least to a doting Dad.)

Humor was always present with Brooke, but she kept it hidden, restrained, so all the more appreciated. Brooke and Caroline could not have been less alike, and their friendship was warm but not close. Brooke's social life was a far cry from Caroline's "Kissing Club", and everyone was staggered when Brooke, in her freshman year at Bowdoin College, fell madly in love with a classmate. This affair, which included a summer together in Europe, lasted two years and had all the semblance of permanence. What ended it, I don't know. Perhaps he was short on humor. Certainly his interests in business were of little interest to Brooke, who had started college as a pre-medical student and ended as an environmentalist. But the parting was friendly and salubrious. It also opened the door for Brooke to meet and take on permanently David James, a graduate of the University of Pennsylvania and the Wharton School, and incidentally, the roommate of one of Caroline's earlier beaux..

The marriage of Brooke and David was what a father dreams of. Two more loving and compatible people cannot be imagined, despite an absolute disparity of interests. David was aptly designed to be a financial officer in business; Brooke, in contrast, started on the road to becoming a doctor (not my doing) but deferred her medical goals until she had borne three children. Then she did an about turn, and chose...nursing! A strange yet fitting occupation for someone of her age and responsibilities. The family lived in Bolton, Massachusetts, a residential semi-countrified town 20 miles west of Boston. On 20 idyllic acres, they built a trout pond, a barn where they bred sheep and donkeys and dogs and chickens. They also planted and reaped the harvest of a vegetable garden that went on and on. And Brooke became the Village Nurse of Bolton, serving it well for 10 years, combining sophisticated medical know-how with community care, and using her skills as a cook to keep her needy patients fed and happy. Most recently she assumed the Village Nurse role in two adjacent villages.

The three James children, Sam (25), Frances (20) and Pete (16) are every bit as caring and nice as their parents. In fact, in my dotage (make that anecdotage) I look forward to the James family becoming the functional center of our tribe. Among other things, Brooke is playing the key role in the continuing care of Caroline, though given an occasional, but important, hand by Eric. This relieves me (and Solange) of much of that responsibility. She is also tending to birthdays and holidays and special events. She keeps the lines of communication open between our far-flung families, particularly when it comes to Melissa Farman's TV appearances. (Melissa is Solange's grand-daughter, and is making a name for herself on stage and screen). Is it any wonder that a most frequent chant heard in our family is: "Thank God for Brooke!"

But don't think for a minute any one of us overlooks Dave, who keeps his fiduciary eye on where our money is going and how much of it is left so we can go on celebrating our good fortune.

Fred's children and siblings

Caroline, Brooke, and Eric

Caroline and Brooke

Chris and Del

Brooke and Caroline

Miles and Chris: twelve years and two feet apart

Chris's Family

Sue 1, Jamie, Kim, Geoff, and Chris

Sue 2

Chris

L to R: Cathy, Kim, Caroline, Jamie, Geoff, Fred. Chris seated. This was his last family portrait.

Chris with Cathy

F.P.H. and C.A.H.

Sue 1 and Caroline, her granddaughter

Kim's daughter, Caroline

Chris on oxygen

Chris backed by grandchildren, and great-grandchildren.
Lee Herter at left.

191

Miles's Family

Miles and Lee at Cheehacombahee

Miles, Lee and their four (Dave, Mike, Neddy, and Caroline)

But what mountain is this, out west?

Latest Miles at Jamie's memorial

Once more, the entire family at Cheehacombahee

Del's Family

Would-be-artist (me) talking to the real thing, Del in her Arizona Studio

Del

Del's daughter, Dové, with her husband, Lee, and their daughter, Cerri

Del and her Clan

Eric's Family

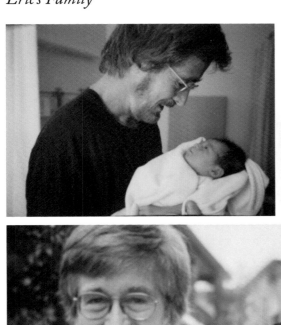

Eric, Hoa and Samantha

Samantha

Eric's Family

With Samantha

With wine

Eric's wife ,Hoa, and daughter, Sam, in Vietnam

Caroline

With younger sister, Brooke, at right

Overcoming a second major illness

Fred's favorite photo of a younger Caroline

Back in the saddle, post-stroke

Brooke's Family

Fred's favorite picture of Brooke and Sam

Brooke and company

Brooke and Sam

Peter with a muppet

Fred and Sam

Brooke's Family

Dave, Brooke and Sam

Sam with a dog

Dave and his trio

Brooke's Family

Sam   *Frances*   *Peter*

Peter, Frances and Brooke

Brooke's Clan

Family Portraits over the years

Manchester, Mass.

Cheehacombahee, South Carolina

Frances's graduation from Concord School

Solange's Family

Solange and Fred with her daughters Jackie, Veronique and Mary, with babies Melissa and Eloise

Nicholas, Morgane and Veronique

Solange's granddaughters, Eloise and Morgane

Theo, Robin, Olive, and Nicholas (Solange's grandsons)

Solange's son Marc, and his children Emily, Josephine and Max

Jackie's children, Jack and Melissa

Melissa and Django

Veronique, Jackie and Solange fooling around

Solange at sea

Solange at ease

Jack

Solange or daughters...can you tell?

Mary, Solange's first born – wow!

Veronique...could she be prettier!

Solange and Fred take to the ocean.

CHAPTER TWENTY-FIVE

ON FOREIGN SHORES WITH SOLANGE

(Breaking My New England Upbringing.
A Spectacular Detour. Back to Beirut.)

Solange and I are now in our 34th year together. We've had a hell of a run, and I guess our only unfulfilled wish would be that of joint parenthood. But Good God! With seven children between us, and fifteen grandchildren, we've had enormous help in filling that void. Divorce on both sides of the aisle presented transient difficulties, but today I can comfortably claim not just compatibility but in large measure, a growing affection between our two families. Even such world-shattering problems such as where Christmas is going to be, or Thanksgiving, or who's going to be at one or the other are surprisingly often resolved without bloodshed!

I'm still astonished, almost every day, at what Solange has done to open my eyes, to expand my interests, and most rewarding, to introduce me to new friends. I simply can't remember, or even imagine, what my life would be without her. For 34 years she has built us a new world, utterly unlike the traditional one of my past. When I think of my proper upbringing, predictably leading to boarding school, followed by Harvard, then carving out a substantial and generally admired career in medicine. I'm apt to claim a solid (some might say 'stolid') life, beyond reproach, but with precious little daily surprise or discovery. Even my momentous involvement with Beirut and the presidency of the American University there, had built-in restrictions. When I wished to be most immersed in the University administration, Lebanon's horrific civil war was erupting. I was kept at arm's length from the actual site of controversy, and was frustrated in my attempts to introduce new measures in education or civil concord. Oh, maybe I did help keep the school stay open during the violence, and had a hand in re-uniting some of the separate segments. But I felt little sense of creation, or of illuminating new pathways to the future. I remain convinced that such attempts must never be abandoned.

Thank God for Solange, with her French/American antecedents, her countless friends throughout the world, her quick intelligence and ready humor, adding life and laughter to every situation. Her deft touch has kept joy a key ingredient in our life. And this has come about without any detectable effort on her part. Yet she inspires, and shows courage, and employs certain innate skills to add fun to her unique recipe for a happy life.

It sounds odd, but she keeps our life so full it's almost hard to find the time to reminisce or recollect our fascinating past. But when I do occasionally dwell on the memory of things past, my thoughts revolve around the strange phenomenon called courage. Or what Hemingway described as 'Grace under pressure.' I think I lacked it early in my career when the surgical department at New York Presbyterian was open for new leadership. I fear I took the easy task of looking good, but avoiding more irksome responsibilities that might place me in a vulnerable position. Was I really good, as a Doctor/Surgeon? Oh, sure, I had developed an agreeable personality. I listened well to patients. And I did, in fact, give extra care for those whose illness called for more than mere surgical skill. But I was never free of the feeling that my patients looked to me with a hope and trust that I couldn't possible fulfill. I was just one person being lavished with the thanks, the love, if you will, from 100 patients. There was a disturbing unbalance in the flow of emotions toward me, which I could hardly return to each patient singly.

It was 100% directed from patient to doctor, and only 1/100% from me back to those patients. I never really learned to solve that dilemma. And it's one of the nagging regrets that I still feel.

Back to Solange and me and our endless voyages. When you think about it, it's no surprise that much of our happy life together involves…Travel! It would take a year to take you along on all our voyages, so I shan't tax your patience with detail and numbers, but I will tell you this: Solange's European acculturation, and my immersion into work in the Middle East, have together fueled the wanderlust of us two natural-born travelers. There are precious few countries that one or both of us haven't visited, and continue to visit, spurred either by work, by family, or simply by falling under the rubric of pure joy.

After I retired from AUB 17 years ago, we suddenly had a surplus of time for travel that didn't depend on vacations or holidays, and, thanks to Great-

Grandpa Charles Pratt and his colleague, John D. Rockefeller, we had the rocks to make such travel comfortable. But these blessings were not of a magnitude to turn us into 'spoiled children'. Both Solange and I had continuing responsibilities...she in the country with her galleries and art world; I with a number of trusteeships. These kept us close to home most of the time.

Solange, of course, was the skipper for most of our voyages, and Paris was often on the first leg of the trip. Her apartment there was home to Solange's family for over three generations. And now it was her daughters, Mary and Jacqueline, with two children each, and four grandchildren, who always had to be visited in their separate Paris homes. But a typical journey might include a stop en route to Les Martins, a tiny village in Provence to hook up with British or American friends, or to Ramatuel on the Mediterranean coast. Solange's mother, Mary, added her own twists to our itinerary. For example, that nudist beach I mentioned earlier. And that time we veered way off course into northern Spain for the sole purpose of seeing the Gehry Guggenheim Museum. It was the most spectacular detour we ever took.

Beirut, our usual goal to the East, was a singular joy. Though we were rarely there during the winter months, we had the advantage of snow in the mountains for skiing in the morning, followed by swimming off the beaches on the same day. Warm weather often had us on the upper plateau, sampling the product of their superior vineyards.

But these journeys were minor when compared to the thrill of living and working at the American University in Beirut. The campus there, with its matchless vistas of sea and mountain is generally considered the most beautiful in the world. We never had trouble inducing the U.S. trustees of AUB to attend meetings there! And within easy driving distance were tempting places to visit. Damascus, in Syria, was only 2 hours away, while Amman, Jordan (even more interesting to me) was almost as easily accessible. Amman's Greco-Roman ruins are among the world's best. Ali Ghandour, a trustee of AUB, is one of Amman's most fascinating citizens and a long-standing friend. Whenever we're in the area, he invites us to dinner at the spectacular Petra (named after St. Peter, Christ's 'rock') which boasts a dramatic entrance beyond compare when approached on horse-back through towering cliffs, then emerging opposite the classically beautiful buildings of the ancient city.

I love her...she loves me!

ADVENTURES WITH MY BIC PEN

(Friendship with Jordon's University and Royalty. A Nervous Night at
Moscow Airport. Joy at Zagorst. Meeting my granddaughter in Vietnam.

As President of AUB, I thought it prudent to befriend my presidential
counterpart at the University of Jordan. So I set up a celebratory event with
him at his school. Why there, and not Beirut? Because Beirut was, to me, the
more prestigious by far of the two universities, I decided it would be both
courteous and friendly, on my part, to allow him the role of host. So there we
met.

Amman's response was overwhelming. The campus was thronged. Everybody
who was anybody in Jordan's capital showed up. There was music and cheering
and applause. After about an hour, the two presidents, hand-in-hand, were
ushered into the imposing 'Signing Room'. We were seated together at a
majestic ceremonial table, with the appropriate 'Friendship' papers before us.
There was a hushed silence while we inked our names under paragraphs that
extolled the present and promised the future closeness of our two schools. We
stood and shook hands, amidst cheers and the popping of flashbulbs. During
the signing, I'd taken note of the elegant gold pen my new academic friend was
using. So I asked for silence, then turned to address my co-signer.

"Mr. President, in my country, whenever a matter of importance between
two parties is solemnified with signatures, tradition has it that the two
signatories exchange pens."

At this point I extended my pen toward him. He looked down at his
priceless gold instrument, then squinted at my 19-cent Bic, then cocked his
head at me, then shrugged at the crowd, and swiftly returned his pen into the
folds of his gown. The whole house roared their applause.

Two years later, Solange and I were invited to an AUB Alumni dinner in
Amman, Jordan. To our delight, we were seated at a table with King Hussein
and Queen Noor. I took the podium after the King and several others had

spoken, and opened with a speech I had used before. A few moments into it I realized it was boring the audience as well as myself, so I threw in the pen story. It got a good laugh, saved my speech, and warmed the crowd. When I returned to the royal table, the King clapped me on my shoulder, then reached under the table and presented me with a gorgeously wrapped package. Now, can you possibly guess? Right you are! An exquisitely wrought gold pen and pencil set. I later discovered that the moment I added the 'pen' story to my speech, King Hussein summoned one of his equerries, whispered something to him, and the equerry did the rest. Proving, once again, as Mel Brooks put it, "It is good to be the King."

AUB alumni affairs also took us to Greece once, and to Russia, twice. The first Russian meeting was between Russian and American academics considered experts about Lebanon's future. I thought that including me, just because of my connection to AUB, was ridiculous. Despite my position, I actually knew little about Lebanon, and the weeklong Moscow meetings often left me in the lurch. On top of that, the Russian group was infinitely better prepared than we were. My major contribution was in seeking out and buying superb Beluga caviar (cheaply) for the U.S. team to take home. And after all, Christmas was on its way.

A residual nightmare from that Russian trip: I arrived at the Moscow airport where I expected to be met by my friend, Richard Murphy, the former U.S. Ambassador to Syria. He was a dependable trustee of AUB, but lacking a bit in timing. There was no one, not a soul, meeting my plane. And I had no idea where I was supposed to live or where I was scheduled to meet for the next seven days. For the next hour I prowled the vast airport, with an increasing sense of hopelessness. I had no names to help me, no phone numbers to call, and only three or four Russian words to guide me. Not a great spot to be in. As the time ground slowly on, I gave up on Ambassador Murphy, but paid increasing attention to a man whom I'm certain had begun to tail me. When this stranger caught up to me and tapped my shoulder, I was sure the jig was up. I turned, and in halting, barely recognizable English, he somehow got across the fact that he was a taxi-driver, and he offered to take me anywhere. But where was anywhere? Two hours later, after stumbling conversation about an American group and a Russian group and an academic center, and after many false leads and dead ends, we ended up at a small institutional-appearing hostelry, near a university. They offered me a bed, but I still had no clue as to where I should be headed. Miraculously, though, they roomed me with a lifesaver: Chinese, yes. English speaking, yes. Occupation, Marine Biologist. Address, Woods Hole, Massachusetts. Woods Hole! Practically my childhood backyard. And best of all, he was fluent in Russian, and for an added treat, he could actually manipulate a Moscow telephone. Oh, happy day!

The next few hours are kind of fuzzy, but somehow he got through to an academic friend, who also knew the Ambassador, and even came up with the name of the hotel where my wife and stepdaughter were arriving the next day, from New York. So by the following noon, I was surrounded by family and Lebanon experts and my new best friend who was Chinese and not only knew the heights of charity but the depth of the ocean! (He got some of my caviar trove, too.)

Maybe to make up for devastating hours of my Russian arrival, there followed one of the most marvelous and moving days of my life. The site was the Zagorsk Monastery, 30 miles north of Moscow. Zagorsk had four separate churches, all open and functioning for the first time since the end of World War ll. They were excitedly waiting the arrival of their Patriarch, head of the Russian Orthodox Church. He was to say Mass in each chapel over the course of the day, each ceremony preceded and followed by choirs of monks and novitiates. Such deep male voices, in precise unison, were of a beauty never before or since equaled in my experience. We were deeply moved. So were the throngs of visitors and parishioners who couldn't attend the monasteries during the war years. We were transported by the experience, and rendered impervious to the bitter cold of that Russian November.

Maybe we didn't feel the cold, but as we left the monastery grounds at dusk, an aging woman, shivering in her shabby rags, approached us, clearly seeking help, or at least a little human warmth. Without a word, Solange took off her own overcoat, and draped it across the poor crone's shoulders. I won't forget, ever, the selfless nature of the gift, and the silent spontaneity of the giver. I'm positive that the woman remembers Solange in her prayers, down to this very day.

Our trip from Zagorsk back to Moscow was also memorable, but in a different sense. We hailed a ramshackle taxi with a headlight that wasn't lit, and a driver who certainly was. Earlier in the day (he told us) he'd had a tooth removed, using lots of vodka as a painkiller. In the darkness (there were no streetlights) the besotted driver lost direction and swerved off the road into the oncoming traffic, crashed through a street sign, and somehow re-crossed the road, ending up on the relative safety of the near shoulder. He was silent, immobile, and seemingly catatonic as we lurched to a stop. We passengers were as speechless with terror as he was.

The car was mortally wounded, and if by any chance the driver had a license, he would most certainly lose it, and, along with that loss, his modus vivendi and livelihood. My attempts to soothe him were not looked on kindly by Solange and Veronique. They were disdainful of the chauffeur, and disgusted with me. I finally got the man to accept a cigarette, and we left him in the dark, smoking away through his tribulations.

The girls, meanwhile, took to the highway, flashing their uncovered legs, ala Claudette Colbert in *It Happened One Night*. And also, just like Miss Colbert, they soon attracted a passing car, to take us, safe and sound, back to Moscow.

For sheer joy (as opposed to academic obligation), who could ever forget Solange's childhood friend, Pat Cavendish, who was our hostess in Cape Town, South Africa. She shared with us her astonishing horse-farm, on a zoo-like plantation of wild animals and birds. Or my pre-Solange photographic safari to Kenya with my 75-year-old mother and my 16-year-old daughter Brooke. This time my tent mate was Bob Hooker, a serious ornithologist. The three blissful weeks of that safari remain a vivid and imperishable memory. Nothing can match the unequaled majesty of the countryside, the Eden-like profusion of flora and fauna, and the discovery that the African starling (unlike ours in New York City) is a winged creature of breathtaking beauty. Not to mention the presence of our personal white hunter, wearing a black eye-patch, the romantic reminder of a previous shooting accident. This near-mythic figure immediately became the object of Brooke's teen-age adoration. What I remember above everything else were the pre-dinner evenings, sitting around an outside fire, drinks in hand and happily trying to identify the cacophony of animal calls and barks and grunts and snarls reaching us through the encroaching darkness We savored the wafting's of dinner in the making, and exchanged thoughts of importance to us. There was no idle chatter. This was heaven!

Where else?

Well, a second trip to Russia, 10 years after the first, but this time, pure pleasure. We traveled from Moscow to St. Petersburg, entirely by inland waterways. And more recently, two week-long cruises, one sponsored by Harvard, when we sailed from Venice to Istanbul, via an interesting jaunt to Palermo, the second embarking from Portugal, and carrying us around the Spanish coast, taking in Casablanca on the way, where both Solange and I echoed Bogart's immortal toast to Ingrid Bergman: "Here's looking at you, kid."

Maybe less romantic, but every bit as fascinating, was an endless trip across the vast Pacific till we reached Hong Kong, and at last our destination: Hanoi, Vietnam. We were there to meet Hoa, Eric's Vietnamese wife and Samantha, the couple's newborn daughter. Samantha is now 13 years old. Two years ago, her schooling was entirely at home, but included 3 months of world travel. One month each was spent in Nepal, Vietnam (her original home), and Bali. Now... was this period away from school and friends a success? Less, I'm afraid than hoped for. Samantha missed her friends, and was much happier to be back with them at her school in Maine. Her schooling has been private, on the Maine coast close to their home in Brunswick, but almost every year she spends a month in Vietnam with her mother. The picture today is quite different. Eric and Hoa are living apart, and Hoa has become a remarkably able teacher of yoga in Brunswick. Samantha meanwhile has been accepted as a live-in student at Cuny College. She will begin her new existence a month from now. Cheers!

If you're still with me, I'll toss in the fact that we made a few short trips to the Caribbean, just to beguile the tedium of a Manhattan winter.

Now I know this list of our sojourns, single or together, would seem to leave little time for more serious endeavors; for me, a career in surgery and education; for Solange, building a successful gallery and dealing in a fascinating art collection. But you must also remember that 33 years is an endless expanse of time, ample to do it all. Especially in the company of the one whose company you treasure best. And I'm here to tell you, each one of those 12,045 days is irreplaceable. Thanks to you, Solange.

Millis, Mass., my favorite farm

Me, Mary and Solange, somewhere in Paris

Looking east from Solange's own mountain

Black Hole Hollow Farm, Upstate, N.Y.

Cheehacombahee, South Carolina. 12,000 acres at one dollar/acre, bought by my grandfather Pratt the day before the 1929 crash

The Parc Monceau, Paris

The glories of East Africa

In Vietnam for a first peek at Samantha, daughter to Eric and Hoa

Pedaling her wares in Hanoi

Ephesus Ampitheater, Turkey

This has to be Morocco and the swimmer has to be me

Halong, Vietnam

World's mightiest oak, Florida

Milady and her consort

CHAPTER TWENTY-SEVEN

DAMN THE TORPEDOS!
FULL SPEED AHEAD!

(Some Dark Days, Some Light. A Few Minor Ills, Plus a Scary One My
Tricks for Longevity. A Tip from Noel Coward.)

Candor compels me to add that these past three years have had their dark days, but after all, what do you expect, given our ages?

Not long after my brother Chris' death in 2007, came daughter Caroline's stroke, then the tumble by Solange, fracturing her pelvic bone, and shortly afterwards, two clumsy falls by me, requiring quadriceps tendon repair and long hospitalization. Finally, and more seriously, my 20-year-old granddaughter, Frances, had a major automobile accident in Kentucky necessitating two operations and long hospital care. Her left eye is functioning less than perfectly, and for her that's a devastating setback, superb skier that she is. But somehow she managed a couple of modest Vermont mountains this past winter, beginning with trepidation, but ending with pure joy.

Just to get back to me, I'm sure you'll be glad to hear that my ten-year-old venous ulcer of the leg (the result of deep vein thrombosis), cum squamous cancer, cum failed skin graft to my left leg, has, at long last, healed! Believe me, that's a monumental relief. An equal blessing is my recently acquired addiction to ice cream. How'd this happen? Well, a year ago I was sentenced to a fortnight in the Saratoga Hospital. The only item on the menu I could tolerate was ice cream…of any flavor. Talk about lucky! It kept me alive, and has remained my fanciful and icy vice ever since.

I've also had an interesting development, non-surgical, but mysterious and almost unheard of. In the summer of 1984, I began behaving increasingly hyperactive. I'd jump up, wide awake, in the middle of the night, my head full of solutions to various problems at the hospital. I'd follow through with visits to the Deans and top administrators. On top of this, I'd write endless esoteric medical papers, or complete chapters for unwritten books, and all this in the dead of night. Some of all this activity made sense, but nevertheless my colleagues noticed all this hyperactivity. To put it nicely, they found it a little odd, and I was beginning to worry about it myself.

This whole episode came to a head in my office one day while I was working with a patient. Out of nowhere, I noticed numbness in both my feet. Then the numbness advanced up legs to my thighs. I was terrified. Suppose the numbness continued...eventually paralyzing my lungs! My heart! My brain! With some effort, I managed to stand, and reach my secretary. She hit the emergency button and within minutes I was on a gurney in the examining room, being poked and probed by every physician available. Slowly, and inexplicably, the numbness reversed itself, and finally stopped.

I was admitted to the hospital. Every test in the book (and a few out of it) was performed in the next days. They revealed nothing. The numbness didn't return, and they sent me home. Their only advice? 'You're suffering from overwork. Take a week off, and worry not.' Easy for them to say.

But Solange and I took their advice. We drove to our farm in upstate New York. Once there I began the arduous job of relaxing. I was on no medication. (All drugs had been cancelled on admission to the hospital.) Then, after three or four days, I was layed low by intense arthritic pain in my neck. I prescribed myself a dosage of Indocin, a drug I'd been taking for several weeks before my hospitalization. The medication brought almost immediate relief. But the next day, when we were out shopping in the little village of Greenwich, I suddenly felt the numbness came back in my feet. This time, no longer terrified, I simply laid myself down on the floor, right in front of curious shoppers and clerks. Within a few minutes, the numbness disappeared, and we drove back home. And on the way, I had an epiphany. The villain was Indocin! There was no other possible culprit.

When I got home, I called Merck, the drug manufacturer of Indocin. They didn't help much. But they did admit that on a couple of occasions, with patients who took high doses of Indocin, over a long period, they did suffer mild and transitory 'neurological symptoms'. Translation: Numbness. I tried to convince Merck to investigate the possibility of separating the hyperactivity side-effect of Indocin from the numbness response. But Merck made no response that I know of. For my part, I struck Indocin off my good list.

I continue to attribute my long life to Lady Luck, buttressed by a full measure of happiness thrown into the mix daily.

I find it totally unbelievable, even preposterous, that my last birthday was my 90th! Ninety years old! Not Mrs. Herter's little boy Freddie! True, I do remember as a young chap setting a goal for myself of surviving for 80 years. I liked the idea that this would squeak me into the next millennium, our current 21st Century. But to live to be ninety is the stuff of dreams.

Could this have happened by intent? What measures (or precautions) did I ever take with longevity in mind?

Absolutely none. Well, almost none. I did heroically give up smoking for good when I hit my eightieth, after over a half-century of addiction. But a lot of other people who kicked the habit too late, are no longer with us. At the hospital, I was known as the surgeon who was the 60 Pack-Year Man. Which translates to a pack a day, every day, for upwards of 60 years. This should have made lung cancer, if not a certainty, at least a strong possibility.

I drank far too much way back in my college days, and continued my evening martini ritual, at least up to last night. I pay no attention to my food intake, nor to whether it is good or bad for me, as long as I like the taste. My children are unanimous in their opinion that I drive too fast, and always have.

And I've had my share of medical problems throughout my long life (only one of which was life-threatening.) My bones and joints have suffered more insults than the average 90-year-old adventurer. And my many scars bear vivid witness to the fact that I'm familiar with both ends of the scalpel. Moreover, the contents of my bathroom cabinet today speak eloquently to the daily needs of various bodily functions.

I continue to give credit for my long life less to Lady Luck than to the happiness I've known, both from loving and being loved. By Solange. By my family. By friends. By having seen, and being part of much of the world. By knowing beauty where it exists, in other people or anywhere else in this ever renewable world. My God, how grateful I feel for these never-ending gifts. And I speak not only of my yesterdays...but of each today, and all the tomorrows to follow.

And I'd like to tell you another reason I give thanks for this blink in the life of the universe that's been given me to share. I've spoken of this earlier, in the Prelude, but it's worth repetition. In wandering through my memories and relating my life story, I've discovered a strange phenomenon. Every time I recall something from my past, another, unbidden memory suddenly pops up. And best of all, this reminiscence works like a telescope. Distant happenings are suddenly brought into sharp focus, and I'm startled by the wealth of detail that the brain retains, decade after decade, episode after episode. The recall of these long-obscured images of family and friends alike have renewed my zest for life and sparked new interest in the everyday adventures that we all, all too often, take for granted.

Not me. Not anymore. From this moment on, I'm determined to follow Noel Coward's sound advice in Tonight at 8:30: "Grab every scrap of happiness you can. Grab every scrap."

And with such friends and family and most of all and always, Solange, that won't be difficult.

So here I am, astride my 90th year, alive and well, taller than most, and possibly more light-hearted than all. Maybe a little handicapped in locomotion, but with every intention of dancing soon again with Solange.

In other words, damn the torpedoes...Full Speed Ahead!

On open sea

One of Solange's birthdays

CHAPTER TWENTY-EIGHT

AN UNABASHED POSTSCRIPT

(The Absolute Best of all my 91 Birthday Parties. My Mansion at Birth.
Tributes to Treasure. Sempre Avanti!)

It would be no less than treasonable to close out this life story without speaking of my 90th Birthday Party.

Solange really should step in now, because it was she who chose the party's location, and made the intricate arrangements, and even decided to whom the invitations should be sent. And all this without a mention to me..not a hint… not a word. But, inveterate snoop that I am around the house, I did pick up a whisper of suspicion of something going on. One friend of hers inadvertently let slip the word 'Brooklyn', but where and why Brooklyn, and what of it, anyway?

The only plausible site for a sizeable dinner, to my mind, was the River Café, at the foot of the Brooklyn Bridge. But I kept my thoughts to myself, and on the fated night, as we drove toward the River Café, we zoomed right past the obvious exit to the restaurant, and drove up Clinton Avenue, where we stopped.

"Look out the window," Solange commanded, "And tell me where we are."

The house number was 229, and suddenly lightning flashed in my brain. This was the house where my grandparents lived, and where I was born and spent the first 3 months of my life! The grand old house still bears the imprint of my great grandfather, Charles Pratt (founder of Pratt Institute) and my grandfather, Frederic Bailey Pratt and his family, happy inhabitants there for half a century. Did I recognize it as we drove up that birthday evening? Well, yes…but only vaguely. I had visited my grandparents there for a short time, but that was 60 years past, and I retained memories of a billiard table in the first floor, but aside from that I had nary a cue.

I was staggered, and stayed so throughout the evening. Close to sixty friends and family arrived…for cocktails, and dinner and speech-making such as I've never heard before. I don't remember a thing that was said, so mesmerized was

I by such endless affirmations of love and praise.

229 Clinton Avenue is two blocks away from Pratt Institute, and I was happy to learn that Tom Schutte, the President of Pratt, now lives there with his wife, and to find that Mitchell (Mike) Pratt, my first cousin, once removed, had been part of the whole evening's elaborate plans. He is now the Chairman of the Trustees of Pratt, continuing the long line of Pratts still involved with the Institute.

Given my age, there were understandably few members of my generation present. But school and college days were brought vividly to life by Dick and Mary McAdoo, standing at the door and, as always, smiling to beat the band. Dick was my roommate at St. Paul's and Harvard, and next to him was Hal Fales, a friend of equal vintage, and all offering poignant songs and stories of our days together through school and college. To recall my long career in medicine, from Harvard Medical School, to my years of teaching and practice at Columbia's Presbyterian Hospital, it took my closest and best pal, the incomparable Fred Jaretzki to sketch in those sixty tumultuous years. But what of the Middle East, and what of the American University of Beirut, both of them occupying all my energies from 1977 till 1993? Well, Nicola and Liz Khuri took care of that, along with two Ambassadors, Dick Murphy of the United States and Jalil Makkawi of Lebanon, along with Alexander Erklentz from AUB's Board of Trustees. Adding still another fillip to this sparkling evening was my treasured friend since college days, Ruth Ellen Dupont.

Ruth had written a marvelous book about her father, Henry Dupont, and about the jewel of his career, the perfecting of Winterthur, his estate, in Wilmington, Delaware, which he had converted into the foremost museum of American furniture in the world. Mr. Dupont was an attractive fellow with endless knowledge concerning furniture, china, and tapestry. But, he was a little short when it same to the ingredients needed to make a mint julep, the drink of choice by a group of us as we lolled around the pond-sized swimming pool one day as guests of Ruth Ellen. We had golfed with her father that morning on his private nine-hole golf course. When I offered my expertise on the manufacture a mint julep, involving seven ingredients in all, he happily put me in touch by phone with his staff in Winterthur's main pantry. I casually enlightened them with this critical information. Not much later, as I sauntered into the pantry to oversee the julep creation, I was flabbergasted to see seven footmen standing tall on one side of an enormous table, each guarding only one of the prescribed contents of the drink. Hemingway had it right: "The very rich are different from you and me."

I'd had a taste of that difference the day before, when Tony Villa and I arrived as Ruth's weekend guests and were escorted to our formidable suite. Once there we were instructed on the whens and wheres of the cocktails and dinner to come. With the brashness and confidence of youth, and dressed to the nines, we left our suite at the appointed hour, and strode off toward the hoped-for gin martinis. Alas, Winterthur, with its maze of rooms, had us in its grasp. We groped about like a couple of blind men until a series of phone calls brought us to the cocktail spot, thirty minutes later, only to see our host and hostess leading the guests to the dining room. Not even a whiff of a martini for us. But we were comforted with many kind words from Ruth Ellen Dupont, bless her, who thought our predicament joyous! (Forgive this fun-to-remember interlude, but my decades of good times with 'Dupy', for Dup-ont, are impossible to forget.)

Two members of the clergy were there, Dean Jim Morton of the Cathedral of St. John the Divine, and Stephen Chinlund, Director of Episcopal Social Services. My two siblings, Adele Seronde and Miles Herter couldn't join us, but a full 22 member contingent of the Herter clan were on lively hand, including my own three children. Caroline couldn't take part in the doings because of her recent stroke, but her ineffable presence brightened the night for me. My son Eric and my daughter Brooke, through their moving prose and poetry, easily compensated for their sister's silence. They were both superb. And my granddaughter, Frances, not surprisingly, took the prize as the most beautiful of the evening's ladies.

But my love, now and forevermore, goes out to Solange. Her characteristically thoughtful, and unfailing imagination in choosing my Brooklyn birthplace for my 90th birthday can never be matched. (At least not for another ten years.)

Fred, 1922, with not much to show...   *Fred, 2012, with nothing to hide*

Ron Holland has had a hell of a life.. so far. In his garishly checkered career he has made a living as a Good Humor man, a Counter-Intelligence Special Agent, a psychiaric aide, an advertising upstart, and these days, editing books. Whatever he's up to, he's always loved hanging around words to see what was going to happen to them.
One could do worse.

Design by Molly Watman, 2012.